THE MAINSTREAM OF WESTERN
POLITICAL THOUGHT

THE MAINSTREAM OF WESTERN POLITICAL THOUGHT

Judith A. Best, Ph.D.

State University of New York at Cortland

 HUMAN SCIENCES PRESS, INC.

Printed in the United States of America
0123456789   987654321

Library of Congress Cataloging in Publication Data

Best, Judith.
  The mainstream of Western political thought.

  Bibliography: p. 143
  Includes index.
  1. Political science—History. I. Title.
JA81.B45   320'.01'091812   LC 80-11042
ISBN 0-87705-271-9
ISBN 0-87705-243-3 pbk.

CONTENTS

PREFACE

Political scientists, historians, and cultural anthropologists habitually speak of the Western political tradition or the mainstream of Western political philosophy. They imply that this mainstream is a coherent tradition, with common concerns, common understandings, and common elements, and that it deals with common problems. Yet students are frequently bewildered by the diverse and contradictory theories they encounter in an introductory survey of Western political thought. Particularly confusing is the apparent dichotomy between ancient and modern thought, a dichotomy that seems to belie the concept of a coherent tradition or mainstream.

Although the common concerns and the common elements are implicit in the classic texts, they are not readily perceived since each great theorist presents a fresh vision of the human experience. Because theorists perceive the world differently, their political prescriptions are fundamental alternatives to each other. What, then, constitutes the Western political tradition? How can we speak cogently of a mainstream of political philosophy? A synthesis is clearly needed. It is hoped that this text, which explicates the tradition, analyzing the quarrels among the philosophers and identifying and assembling the accords, may provide the coherence that would otherwise be missed.

Chapter 1

WESTERN POLITICAL PHILOSOPHY
The Quest

Bold Lover, never, never canst thou kiss,
though winning near the goal—yet, do not grieve;
she cannot fade, though Thou has not thy bliss,
Forever wilt thou love, and she be fair.

John Keats

The word *philosophy* comes from the Greek philos, meaning to love or the love of, and sophia, meaning wisdom. Philosophy means the love of wisdom. Lovers, so the poets tell us, ardently pursue the object they love, seek a perfect unity with what they love, and yet in a certain sense, all are doomed to failure, since each physical phenomenon is unique and distinct. There are practical limits to a blending, a mixture of the lover and the loved, but this is what makes loving so enticing. As Mark Twain observed, to make a man want something it is only necessary to make it difficult to obtain.

A feeling of incompleteness and an urgent attraction to something outside oneself makes the lover a pursuer, a seeker. Philosophy, the love of wisdom, is thus a quest, and *political philosophy* is a quest for knowledge about political things, a sustained quest using human reason to hunt for understanding about man, society, and government. Political philosophy asks, What is man? What is the best way for a man to live? How can men best live together? Since each of us has but one life to live, these questions are of the first order. There are, however, profound disagreements about the answers to these questions. Political philosophy is an activity and a process, not a series of dogmatic answers.

The history of Western political philosophy has been characterized by a number of basic quarrels among the political philosophers: quarrels about the concept of nature—what nature means and how it can and should be used; quarrels about the concept of man—what he is, what he needs, and what he wants; quarrels about the concept of government—what roles government should play, what goals it should pursue, what limits should be placed on the exercise of its power. Each political philosopher has an original perspective on these questions. Each makes a unique contribution to the tradition of Western political thought. No philosopher agrees completely with any other political philosopher about the answers to the fundamental questions. The fact, however, that each has a novel point of view appears to controvert the coherence of the tradition of Western political thought. The contradictions among the diagnoses of philosophers, and the diversity of their prescriptions are so immediately evident that the integrality of the tradition seems to dissolve; the whole disintegrates into its parts.

In an effort to avoid individualized segmentation and to organize and classify these contributions, Western political philosophy is commonly divided into two periods, *classical* or *ancient thought* and *modern thought.* Ancient thought begins in the fifth century B.C. with the Athenian, Socrates; modern thought begins in the sixteenth century A.D. with the Florentine, Machiavelli. This division is both logical and useful for it draws attention to a fundamental disagreement about political things, a disagreement that shapes and unites the political prescriptions of each period.

Each of these two periods represents a distinct and identifiable perspective on man and on politics. It is a commonplace of theoretical analysis, for example, that ancient political thought is characterized by an emphasis on excellence and inequality, and that modern political thought is characterized by an emphasis on freedom and equality. Within limits, such generalizations frame our understanding, acknowledge affinities among the philosophers within a period and confirm contrasts among the philosophers of different periods. Because the ancient/modern dichotomy depicts actual substantive differences between the groups of philosophers, generations of students have found it to be a helpful analytical model.

No doubt, opposition is a useful method of definition and analysis. For example, our comprehension of Christian theology is enlightened by our recognition of the Catholic/Protestant dichotomy, and more specifically by the fact that Protestantism began as a rejection of and rebellion against certain established principles of Catholic theology. Christianity is, nonetheless, a coherent tradition, a tradition that transcends a Catholic/Protestant dichotomy that concentrates solely on the differences between the two groups and ignores their fundamental agreements.

Despite its analytic serviceability, the ancient/modern dichotomy, like the Catholic/Protestant dichotomy, is a distinction that can be overdrawn. Western political philosophy, like Christianity, is a coherent tradition, a complex whole. By focusing too narrowly and too exclusively on the antithetical features of the tradition, one can lose sight of its unifying characteristics. Analysis must be followed by synthesis; the elements of a tradition once isolated and classified must finally be reassembled lest the harmony, the concordance of the tradition be obscured.

A major goal of a final synthesis is to identify the basic principles that animate the mainstream of the tradition, to discover its dominant ideas. Once ascertained, the principles of the mainstream bridge the ancient/modern dichotomy, connecting the philosophers of each period in a joint endeavor. Every living, coherent tradition has a mainstream. Christianity's major congruence is to be found in a belief in the divinity of Jesus of Nazareth. Catholics and Protestants of the mainstream of Christianity are united on this fundamental principle. It constitutes the chief and controlling thrust of Christian thought. Christianity also has a crosscurrent, a subsidiary, diverging theme. Thus, among Christian sects are those who follow the teachings and aspire to the example of Jesus, although they do not affirm his divinity.

Western political philosophy has a mainstream and a crosscurrent. Despite the significant disagreements among them, the ancient and modern philosophers of the mainstream agree on a number of central, elemental concepts, concepts that set the primary and distinctive direction of the tradition. These points of agreement, from the perspective of the whole, are of greater consequence than the points of disagreement. The quality of the tradition, making it such as it is, is grounded on these shared ideas. The subsidiary ideas, the principles of the crosscurrent, while influential and important in themselves, are not controlling, are not dominant, but rather are ancillary to the tradition as a whole. Thus, they may serve as a counterpoint that offsets and illuminates the primary principles—the principles of the mainstream.

The chapters that follow are written to provide a synthesis of Western political philosophy, a synthesis that explicates and reunites its various elements, distinguishing its major thrust, the mainstream, from its ancillary course, the crosscurrent. Each master theorist does have an original perspective on the nature of political reality. There are significant and consequential differences between ancient and modern political thought. In order to answer the question, What constitutes the Western political tradition?, these quarrels must be explained and transcended. The parts must be reassembled so that the complex whole is revealed. The uniqueness and variety of the trees fascinates and captures the imagination, but in the end we must be able to see the forest and not just the trees. We must be able to see the whole, which is greater than any of its parts. The principles of the mainstream are the major object of the inquiry because they dominate the whole tradition, fix its direction, and express its cardinal concepts.

Although the crosscurrent functions within the tradition in a supplemental and secondary capacity because it transvalues the whole, and because its evaluations and prescriptions are based on principles at variance with the accepted standard, it is, nonetheless, a part of that tradition. It is a part of the Western political tradition because it addresses the same questions, the timeless questions about the meaning or purpose of human life. It too asks, what is the good life? How can men live well? All the great theorists of the tradition have sought a comprehensive knowledge of the whole. They all have claimed to possess some insight into the universal values, the true, proper, or final goals of man. In short, each has attempted to define human happiness and has prescribed a way to obtain it. Happiness is the final end of man; it is the term we give to complete human fulfillment or the human good. Happiness is then the value of values. But, what is happiness? What are the highest values and how do we obtain them?

Each and every political philosopher has pursued these questions—human values and the means of achieving them are the subject matter of political philosophy. Socrates, for example, analyzed the intrinsic worth of justice. In *The Republic,* he attempts not only to define justice, but also to determine whether it is beneficial and if so for whom. In order to appraise justice simply, justice and nothing else, Socrates and his companions examine the life of the man who is stripped of all other apparently desirable things. They examine the life of the man who has justice and nothing else. Since happiness is the human good, the test for justice is the comparative happiness of the perfectly just man and the perfectly unjust man. Therefore, the question Socrates' companions put to him was: Who is happier, the unjust man who is rich, honored, loved, and who has the appearance of being just, or the just man, who is poor, scorned, unloved, and appears to be unjust?[1]

Asking questions and testing the validity of answers by their consistency, comprehensiveness, and congruity with reality, in a word *dialectic,* is the original operational mode of political philosophy. Doubt about the complete and final valid-

ity of any and all answers is the original operational mood of
political philosophy. The mode, dialectic, and the mood, doubt,
produce answers in the form of ideas that are all to a certain
extent provisional because they are not sufficiently comprehensive. Dialectics is a process in which a question is raised and
answer offered. This answer or idea is called the *thesis.* To test
the validity of the thesis, more questions are raised and arguments proffered that culminate in a counteridea called the *antithesis.* The thesis and the antithesis are at a tension with each
other, and the attempt to resolve the tension raises new questions and new arguments that if successful produce a third idea,
the *synthesis,* which incorporates and transcends both the thesis
and the antithesis. For example, in *The Republic,* one of the
participants, a famous rhetorician, advances the idea that justice is the advantage of the stronger.[2] After listening to an
argument for and a discussion of this thesis, another participant
in the debate, Plato's brother, suggests the counteridea that
justice is the advantage of the weaker.[3] The incompatibility of
these two ideas, each of which is based on or drawn from some
human experience, is the prod to a synthesis, another idea, a
larger or higher idea of which the thesis and the antithesis are
mere parts. For example, the idea that justice is not simply and
purely advantageous to anyone. The dialectical process can
continue because doubt as to the completeness and finality of
the third idea results in new questions, and thus a synthesis is
converted into a new or second thesis.

The process of examining ideas by question and answer is
not simply an interesting intellectual exercise. It has enormous
practical, political consequences because its product is political
prescription. The founders of our regime, for example, asked
themselves, What is the legitimate purpose of government?
They answered, To increase human freedom, and they defined
human freedom in terms of the responsiveness of government
to the will of the governed. Freedom in the form of responsiveness was one of their primary ideas. No sooner is this idea
established than a counteridea occurs, the idea of stability.

American
Regime

However highly we value freedom, we cannot forget about stability, the continued existence of the government, the steadiness of the law as the means of securing freedom. Stability is necessary because men cannot obey laws they cannot know, and they cannot know laws that change continuously. Indeed, without some degree of stability, law, which is a general rule, disappears and is replaced by fiat. Without stability, men are enslaved to the moment; no great and longterm enterprises can be undertaken because a man cannot rationally predict that what he builds today will not be torn down tomorrow. On the other hand, stability limits freedom. To the extent that we value or opt for stability, we circumscribe the will of the governed. As a matter of constitutional policy, stability requires long terms in office so that those who begin projects can complete them. But, freedom requires short terms in office so that the people may remove officials at their pleasure. Freedom the idea, stability the counteridea, and the founder's suggested synthesis, liberty or liberty under law, produced a constitutional system in which the will of sustained and durable majorities must prevail in the long run, though not necessarily in the short.

Dialectics is a process that broadens and deepens our understanding, but it also is a process that creates doubt, invites debate, and reaps dispute. The original operational mode and mood of political philosophy seem to have set indelible marks upon the whole tradition. Doubt, debate, and dispute characterize the "dialogue" of the Western political philosophers. The master political philosophers do not agree on what the highest ends are or on how we may attain them. Their answers are contradictory, their ideas are alternatives to each other. The history of political philosophy is in itself evidence that there are a variety of ends or values for man and that these ends or values are frequently in conflict. On the other hand, the history of political philosophy indicates that there is a hierarchy of values. From Socrates, who saw a conflict between two very high things, philosophy and the law, to Nietzsche, who saw the conflict between truth and life, each philosopher has ultimately agreed that there is a hierarchy of values. And so, though Socrates taught moderation and attempted to reconcile or mitigate the tension between philosophers and the city, he found philosophy to be higher than the law. So Nietzsche found life to be higher than truth. So Locke and Rousseau declared freedom to be the highest value. So Tocqueville and Aristotle preferred excellence to equality.

While the philosophers of the Western political tradition have differed in the precise placement of values in a hierarchy, they have agreed that there is and must be a hierarchy. They maintained that not every value system can pass the bar of reason, not every human activity or goal is equally desirable and praiseworthy. These are men who came to the political process to praise and to blame, men who want to distinguish good regimes from bad regimes, to learn what makes good regimes good and bad regimes bad, and thereby to improve the bad ones and to maintain the good ones. They are the physicians of the political process who diagnose disease and prescribe remedies to regain health. Like physicians of the body, they must know what health is and must recognize its superiority to disease. In short, they agree that there is an objective answer to the question, What is the best way to live?

Political philosophy is classified as a field in the social sciences, but it is not just one field among many, it is the architectonic field. The architect has the vision of the whole: he knows how the finished product should look and function. Because of this, the architect can direct all of the expert artisans, bricklayers, electricians, carpenters, and plumbers. The cooperative effort of the artisans is purposive and productive only because there is an architect, someone who can transcend their individual skills and direct and coordinate their activity. This architectonic role of analyzing and explicating values, of providing a vision of an ordered whole, is performed for the discipline of political science by political philosophy.

The practical value of the social sciences is to find a means to achieve given ends. For this purpose the social sciences have to understand the ends, to know what they are. This is particularly true of the "Queen" of the social sciences, politics. Politics is goal oriented. All political action is guided by some thought of better or worse. Thought of better or worse implies the idea of the good simply, a knowledge of the good life and the good society. Knowledge of the good simply is the holy grail that political philosophy seeks. Political philosophers attempt to discover not only what is, but also what ought to be. Political philosophy is a quest for the true ends of man; it is an attempt by serious men to capture a rational nonarbitrary standard, a standard that allows us to judge whether our regime is noble or base, a standard that permits us to distinguish between human excellence and human depravity, a standard that serves as a goal toward which our energy may be directed. We can work toward practical solutions to the social problems of our time, we can select sensible and proper means only if and only because we have some understanding of our objectives, some insight into the timeless values and of the tensions and contradictions among them.

Political philosophy is a very old discipline, and although it is an ongoing activity, it has been going on for enough centuries to make a progress report a legitimate demand. What does the discipline of political philosophy have to teach us? What can students of politics today learn from the study of so many radically differing and often ancient analyses of man and his society? Why not simply focus our study on the most recent theories or those most widely accepted in our time and relegate the study of the master philosophers of the past to antiquarian historians?

Perhaps the best way to answer these questions is to state at the outset what we do not learn from the study of political philosophy. We do not learn the gospel, we do not learn which theory, which comprehensive vision of the whole is simply true, nor which theories are false and heretical blasphemy. What we can learn from political philosophy is to know what it is that we do not know, to realize that we are ignorant about the most important things. Knowledge of ignorance, said Socrates, is the beginning of wisdom. If he is right, then the enterprise of political philosophy is well underway. To realize that we are ignorant about the most important things is to understand that the one needful thing is to continue the quest for knowledge about the most important things.

Man is the creature who asks, Why? The discipline of political philosophy seeks not only to introduce us to the master theorists but also to introduce us to ourselves. If we hope to learn who we are, what we are, and even what we are for, we too must engage in the expedition, continue the quest. We begin by inspecting and sorting out our own values, by learning to recognize our inconsistencies and contradictions, and by testing our ideas and experience against the enduring and timeless ideas of the great thinkers of the past. Through the ages men have retreated to deserts, roamed the earth in search of themselves, and our age is no exception. "I've got to find myself!" is the perennial cry. Political philosophy offers us an alternative method of self-acquaintance. It takes us not to the wilderness but to the forum, it engages us in debate rather than sightseeing, it makes us participants rather than spectators.

If the lives of men are to have any meaning, if men are not so many "flies of a summer," if men have needs and desires *and purposes,* then political philosophy is necessary to provide a basis for understanding and prescription. The political philosophers have analyzed and dissected man and his society searching for his proper goals. They have examined the origins and the ends of government. They have described the tensions between the individual and the group, between freedom and equality, between virtue and peace, between justice and excellence. Their very disagreements demonstrate the rich variety and complexity of the creature that is man, and thereby enlarge our horizons, challenge conventional ways of looking at the world, and permit us to discover the fundamental political problems.

Although the political philosophers have quarreled about the answers to the fundamental questions, they have examined the *same* problems, and their prescriptions comprise the fundamental alternatives, the limited set of answers for serious men. The "right" answer is illusive, the quest unending, for philosophy, like life, is an activity and a process, dynamic not static, a debate not a recitation. As Santayana has observed, "all problems are divided into two classes: soluble questions which are trivial and important questions which are insoluble." Political philosophy teaches us how to distinguish between these two classes of problems. It teaches us the scope and limits of politics. It trains us to recognize the universal in the particular, permitting us to distinguish "the pastness of the past as well as its presence." The ultimate apology for political philosophy is not that it provides us with the right answers, but rather that it provides us with the right questions.

Chapter 2

THE ANCIENTS
The Discovery of a Standard

Hardly anybody, expect possibly the Greeks at their best, has
realised the sweetness and glory of being a rational animal.

George Santayana

Evaluation of political phenomena is a primary task of
political philosophy. When we evaluate anything we need a
standard, an established measure of quantity, quality, capacity,
range, or value. If we would know whether one man is faster
than another, we select units in time and space and thus can say
of one man that he runs 100 yards in 10 seconds and of the other
that he runs the same distance in 15 seconds. And, if we would
evaluate political things, if we would distinguish between free
states and slave states, for example, if we would establish the
superiority of one to the other, we must have a standard. So,
the first task of political philosphy is to discover the criteria that
shall be used in evaluating political things.

The search for a political standard is a difficult and complex project in part because political philosophy attempts to
make qualitative assessments rather than merely quantitative
ones. Ultimately, political philosophy is not concerned with
how large in territory a state may be, or with how many citizens
a state possesses, or even how many people voted in a given

election. These may be interesting and even useful questions, but they are not the ultimate or final questions. Thus, they are not the concern of political philosophy. Political philosophy attempts to discover and distinguish the quality of regimes, their essential character, their degree of excellence, their relative goodness.

Quality is not easy to measure because we have great difficulty in agreeing on what is an appropriate unit of qualitative measurement. This is not the case with quantitative assessments. The units are simple, defined, established, and commensurable. If we wish to measure weight, we use grams, ounces, and pounds. Our only concern is the accuracy of our measurements. But what are the qualitative units of measurement? What are their names, and what do they represent? We all can name many possible standards for evaluating political things: liberty, equality, fraternity, excellence, prosperity, stability, independence. Which is the most appropriate or useful standard? How do these standards relate to each other? In measuring length, we can readily use inches or feet or yards or a combination of them all because they are commensurable: a foot is always a third of a yard, an inch always one-twelfth of a foot. However, the terms of political evaluation are not commensurable. Indeed, they are often incompatible and contradictory. Liberty and equality are frequently at a tension with each other. What then is a proper combination or proportion of the two? What is the appropriate standard of political evaluation?

Another complicating factor in the evaluation of political things is the necessity of discovering a universal and unchanging standard. This is a problem shared by all kinds of evaluation including quantitative measuring systems. Although quantitative measuring systems differ from one regime to another (length in the United States is measured in inches and feet whereas in other regimes it is measured in centimeters and meters), the units themselves are universal and unchanging. An inch everywhere is one-twelfth of a foot or 2.54 centimeters.

Uniformity and consistency of the units of measurement

are the bedrock of science. As G. K. Chesterton observed in his essay "Science and the Savages,"

> Men can construct a science with very few instruments, or with very plain instruments; but no one on earth could construct a science with unreliable instruments. A man might work out the whole of mathematics with a handful of pebbles, but not with a handful of clay which was always falling apart into new fragments, and falling together into new combinations. A man might measure heaven and earth with a reed, but not with a growing reed.

The uniformity and consistency of its units of measurement make quantitative evaluation relatively simple. Science, understood in this context as the discipline that relies upon quantitative measurement, has this advantage over political philosophy, an art whose standards are not as tractable and manageable. Men do not quarrel over the extent of an inch or a centimeter, but they do quarrel over such measurements as stability, freedom, equality, and excellence. The units of qualitative evaluation are not as easily handled as the units of quantitative analysis. Like Chesterton's handful of clay, they "are always falling apart into new fragments, and falling together into new combinations." Nonetheless, political philosophers have sought a universal and unchanging standard by which to appraise the quality of political things.

The earliest political philosphers, the ancients, found such a standard in the concept of nature. Political philosophers cannot claim to be the discoverers of the concept of nature. Political philosophy is preceded by philosophy itself, and nature is the subject matter of philosophy. As the original philosophers observed the world around them, they noted that some things exist in or act in the same way. For example, fire everywhere needs air to burn. The first philosophers were natural scientists who probed and discovered the natures of things. The *nature* of a thing is its particular intrinsic character, its fundamental qualities, its truest essence, the way it looks, the way it acts.

And its character is not made by man, its essence is not controlled by man, its way is not determined by man. This concept of nature, like all basic ideas, manifests its own antithesis, the concept of the artificial or conventional, that which is made by man or which is because men posit it. Things are either by nature or by art, by the intervention and creative activity of man. A tree is by nature, though a man can plant a tree; chairs and tables are by art, though a man uses a natural object as a tree to make them. The Greek word for nature is physis, meaning growth—trees grow, chairs and tables do not.

The concept of nature also makes apparent a second antithesis, the *supernatural*, the sacred, that which is made by the gods, attributable to some divine agency or miraculous intervention. Roses grow; they are by nature, but roses growing in the snows of a bitter winter are contrary to the way or nature of roses, and thus supernatural as occurring outside of the characteristic order of roses. The concept of nature lies in the middle, as a kind of mean between the supernatural and the *artificial*. Things that are natural are not made things, and thus they are not made by either gods or men.

But nature is not simply a mean, it is also a state of completion and fulfillment for the nature of a thing is its truest essence, its highest manifestation, its apex of existence. The Greek word for nature, *physis*, means not only growth, but that into which a thing has grown when it is complete. An acorn is by nature, but if you would know the nature of an acorn, you must know what it is for, what it is destined to become, what it is meant to be. The perfect oak is the nature of acorns. Not every acorn grows into the perfect oak or even into an imperfect oak. Some oaks are scraggly, misshapen, or diseased, but the nature of a thing is to be found in its particular excellence not in its average. Therefore, to say a thing is natural in this sense is to praise it, and the term natural is a term of distinction and superiority.

Finally, the concept of nature is a concept of limitation. Nature means growth, and the perfection of growth, but there are certain limits to growth. To say what the way or character of a thing may be is to say that there are boundaries to growth and to being. Nature is not only a goal to be achieved, it is a restraint on what may be achieved. Thus, an acorn is destined to be an oak: it may grow into a scraggly oak or the perfect oak, but it is confined to being an oak. It cannot grow into a rose; it cannot grow into a man. The concept of nature circumscribes reality, yielding at one and the same time the extent of possibility and impossibility. To summarize, nature is:

1. The peculiar characteristics of a thing.
2. Not made either by men or gods.
3. The peculiar excellence of a thing.
4. A limitation on being.

Artificial or conventional things can also be said to have their ways or customary manifestations, and even their own peculiar excellences. Shoes, for example, are made things. Their particular way or custom is to protect feet while at the same time permitting the feet to function. Shoes are made things, they are by art, but feet are by nature. Shoes are designed for many different conventional functions, from toe dancing to soccer playing. Shoes take many different forms, but they are always secondary phenomena. Shoes are for feet, and feet are by nature.

The adoption of nature as a *standard* occurred in part because of nature's priority. Things that are by nature are givens. They are necessary conditions or circumstances of art and convention. This state of being first in time lends a primacy to the natural that alone would make it a candidate for the job of standard. But, nature as a concept possesses other attributes that lend credence to its adoption as a standard.

Nature's purposiveness qualifies it as a standard. As an ideal or state of ultimate perfection, the criteria necessary to make judgments are located within or are intrinsic to the concept. As the highest manifestation of a thing, nature is not only an ideal or a goal, but also a termination and thus an end—a final excellence. Because the perfect oak is the end or final excellence of acorns, the perfect oak is the rule and measure of all acorns and oaks.

Furthermore, the natural *as the natural simply* is universal and unchanging. Fire burns everywhere the same. Once we identify the custom or way of a thing, we have identified the characteristics common to all the individual cases. The genus dog has many and various species, but all dogs walk on four legs, or it is in the nature of dogs to walk on four legs. This is a universal and unchanging characteristic of dogs. This is not to say, however, that no dog has ever walked on three or two legs, for observation tells us that some dogs have done so. Accident has left some dogs mutilated, and all of us who have seen a circus have seen dogs trained to walk on two legs. The natural four-legged gait of circus dogs is sublimated by the trainer. The fact that men can by art restrain, divert, or harness nature does not necessarily mean that men can change the concept of the natural. Circus dogs may walk on two legs, but they do not do it well. The amazing thing is that they do it at all. Men cannot substitute or replace the natural characteristics of the thing. Men can change conventional things. They can change the value of paper money as an act of will, but they cannot convert an onion into an orange. Things that are natural possess their ways or customs independently of human endeavor and human decision. Despite the performance of circus dogs, it remains in the nature of dogs to walk on four legs. The very fact that we are willing to spend money and time watching circus dogs perform is in itself evidence that we recognize such activities as unnatural, rare, and freakish. No one spends money to watch dogs walk on four legs. The fact that nature is unchanging in this sense, the fact that it is not made by man and thus cannot be changed by man, makes it a reliable instrument of evaluation. Nature as a standard is not subject to human whim and will, nor to human caprice or prejudice.

The ancient political philosophers' arguments for nature as a standard, in the main, are: its *reliability*—because of its universality and unchangeableness; its *rigor*—because of its terminal excellence; and its *cogency*—because of its priority to art and convention.

THE NATURE OF MAN—THE STANDARD REFINED

Reliability, rigor, and cogency, however, do not quite suffice. Propriety is also essential: a standard must be suitable to the thing evaluated. The concept of nature is too large, too all-encompassing to serve as a standard for political things. If we are interested in the development of oaks, we do not set out to measure forests, for forests are often composed of many dissimilar kinds of trees, trees whose ways of development are very different from oaks. Sometimes it is necessary to see the trees rather than the forest. This recognition that nature is a whole composed of essentially different parts led the first political philosopher, Socrates, to refine the distinction between nature and convention in order to find an appropriate standard for measuring political things. The standard Socrates introduced was the *nature of man*. As natural phenomena, the things of the heavens and the things of the earth have their own ways. Man is a natural being, and, according to Socrates, his way is different from the way of the stars and planets, and the way of oaks and roses.

Politics is the art of governing men or the science of managing the public affairs of men, and thus the nature of man is the appropriate standard for these human activities. A philosophical anthropology is the foundation stone of political philosophy. Every political theory is based on a theory of human nature. Every political philosopher has asked, What is man? What is the specific difference between men and all the other natural phenomena? Since the nature of man is the standard for political things, any disagreement about the nature of man or about the substance of the standard accounts for the differences in evaluation and prescription among the political philosophers. The quarrels about political philosophy can be traced to one source—a disagreement about the nature of man. We are the object we study, and this has advantages and disadvantages. That cool and sober detachment, with which a man can study a rock or insect as totally foreign and separate from his own being, may be impossible, but the direct awareness and the immediacy of knowledge with which a man can study his own species may provide a depth of understanding not possible in the study of rocks and insects. A man does know what it is to be a man in a way he cannot know what it is to be an insect.

The tradition we call Western political philosophy begins with an agreement that the nature of man shall serve as the standard for measuring political things. The earliest political philosophers, the ancients, defined the nature of man in terms of *rationality.* Man is the rational animal. Nature, said Aristotle, does nothing in vain, and it has given man speech and reason.[1] Speech is unique to man among the animals—only man has a true language. Speech and reason presuppose each other. Man reasons because he has speech, and he speaks because he can reason. Speech and reason are purposive; they allow men to distinguish the just from the unjust, the virtuous from the vicious; they allow men to probe and consciously apprehend the ordered whole.

The fact that animals do communicate with each other does not deny the uniqueness of man's rationality and language. Animals use sounds to signify presence, danger, pleasure, pain, or fear to each other. But, animals cannot ask for reasons; animals cannot advance reasons. If one dolphin can signal to another, "come with me," another dolphin can signal "yes" or "no," but cannot ask "why should I?" Animals can communicate the *what* of a situation: I live in this tree; I am your mate; a predator is near. Men are the creatures who not only can ask Why? What is the motive? the cause? the explanation? the justification?, but astoundingly, men are the creatures who often can answer these questions.

Man is by nature the rational animal, and the concept of

nature means the highest manifestation of a thing, its fulfillment and completion. However, observation tells us that all men are not equally rational or rational all of the time. Man is not simply rational; he is also passionate. Like the arational animals, he feels as well as thinks; his soul has three parts: the desiring, the spirited, and the rational.[2] The highest part of the soul, or the rational part of man is his specific way, and therefore, it is higher than the body and the other parts of the soul because it is more specifically human, more natural to man. Using nature as the standard, it is incumbent upon a man to develop his reason.[3] In a healthy man the rational soul rules the whole being, or the most natural man is the most rational man.

Reason is purposive; it has a product. Reason allows a man to distinguish good from evil, and, therefore, man's rationality makes him a moral animal—one capable of living a virtuous life. The pleasures and pains of the body and the passions that move animals are not the only things that can move men. Rationality allows men to distinguish among bodily pleasures and pains, to distinguish among the passions and to determine which pleasures and pains, which passions are good and which are bad. A man who might find rape pleasurable can rationally determine that it is bad, and can overrule the apparent pleasure of the body. Or, a man whose body gags at bitter medicine may rationally determine that the medicine is good for the body, not bad as it appears to be. His mind will then compel his body to accept it.

Shakespeare put this ancient understanding of the nature of man most succinctly saying, "What a piece of work is a man! How noble in reason!" Human excellence and worth are to be found *in,* as a part, characteristic or property of reason. Rationality allows men to perceive the difference between the apparent and the real good. It frees men or permits them to choose the noble over the base. Because the peculiar excellence of man is rationality, he can live the good life, the life in accordance with virtue. The happiness of man is to be found in the good life.[4]

Chapter 3

THE ANCIENTS

Political Things are Natural

The spirit of a government must be that of the country. The form of a government must come from the makeup of the country. Government is nothing but the balance of the natural elements of a country.

José Martí

The first political philosophers, Socrates, Plato, and Aristotle, the ancients, adopted the concept of the nature of man as the criterion for evaluating political things. Therefore, the first fundamental question they raised about politics was, Are political things natural? To the extent that political things are natural, they are, according to the ancient political philosophers, good—excellent, beneficial and praiseworthy.

Aristotle, the first political scientist, the first political philosopher to give us a formal, systematic account of politics on its own grounds, teaches that the political community is natural.[1] Bearing in mind that the concept of nature means the highest or truest manifestation of a thing, the natural political community is not any and every political community, but rather is the most perfect political community. Aristotle calls this natural political community the *polis*.[2]

Before we can analyze Aristotle's teaching that the polis is natural, we must first determine what a polis is. A polis is a species of association, a body of persons united for a common purpose. It is the highest, most sovereign, most inclusive and most self-sufficient association. All of us belong to many different kinds of associations, a family, a team, a church, a fraternity, a club. Frequently, one association is part of another larger association. A professor of political philosophy is a member of a political science department, which is a part of a social sciences division, which is a part of a college, which may be a part of a university, and which may be part of a state educational system. Each higher association includes within its own end the end of the lesser association it assimilates, and so the final association, in this case, a state educational system, has the broadest, most inclusive end or goal.

Since the polis is the most inclusive association, it is not and cannot be the equivalent of the modern term the state. The modern term state is not an all-embracing term as our distinctions between church and state or between society and state indicate. As we understand the terms, state and church have essentially different purposes even though on occasion they interact. Our terms state and society distinguish the apparatus or administration of government from the rest of the community life. These distinctions are foreign to the concept polis, a primary term representing an internal organic wholeness for which we have no real equivalent in our language. The closest we can come to approximating it is our word country. If you meet a man while traveling around the world and ask him who he is, his most common reply is: I am an American, a Frenchman, a Spaniard, a Russian. He identifies himself with his country, not his state, his religion, his occupation, his party or even his hobbies. A man does not say, I am a citizen of a democratic republic, a citizen of a totalitarian dictatorship, a Lutheran, a Buddhist, an ironworker, a carpenter, a socialist, a monarchist, a golfer, or a stamp collector. He says, I am Canadian, I am Italian. He says this because he expects it to be generally informative, and indeed it is, for we know a great deal about a man when we know his country.

Specifically, what is it that we know? What does this invocation of country tell us that the other means of identification do not? It tells us about a *complete* way of life. A man's country is not simply a geographical place; it is not simply land, language, and law, though these are the three core elements. It is also a community of beliefs, attitudes, and experiences that arise from a common heritage and look toward a shared future. It is an habitual and customary manner and style, and so we speak of the British way of doing things, of Chinese art, of Greek architecture, of German philosophy, of French literature, of American food. A country is a common horizon, a way of life that is full, that lacks nothing, that includes in some particular form everything that a man needs to be happy.

When we say, "That's as American as apple pie or the Fourth of July," we are drawing attention to a total environment. To say "That's as American as baseball" does not mean that we all play baseball or even enjoy it. It means that baseball is one of those things that affects our common existence, is a condition of our group experience, of our collective memories. In America, one cannot read a newspaper or watch television without being confronted by baseball; one cannot drive by a park, watch children play, attend an organizational picnic without seeing, hearing, or participating in baseball. Enthusiast or not, it is almost inconceivable to imagine an American who has not heard of baseball because it is part of our culture, the sum total of our behavior patterns, the interrelated whole we call our country.

If we can understand the term country in this larger sense of a complete way of life, we may begin to understand (not as an equivalent, but as an approximation) Aristotle's polis as the complete association, the self-sufficient community, the final community because it lacks nothing. All associations of men, Aristotle points out, aim at some good because an association is a product of an intentional human action, and all intentional human actions are directed toward some good.[3] Although this premise that all intentional human actions are directed towards some good seems to be naive, it actually is a matter of common sense, if we make a distinction between real and apparent goods. A man eats because he is hungry, that is the relief of hunger seems to him to be a good thing. If a man takes the wrong action, it is not because he seeks some evil, but rather because his judgment, his rationality, is weak or mistaken. The man who eats too much and becomes fat or develops indigestion has suffered from a failure of judgement. The masochist who seeks pain does not do so because he thinks pain is undesirable but because he mistakenly enjoys it. Even the suicide aims at some good, the absence of physical or mental anguish—oblivion.

The good that is the target of intentional human action may be merely an apparent good, a mirage, not a real good, and this men have learned through all ages to their sorrow. The real good in human terms is *happiness*—the good life, or as Aristotle discovers in *The Nicomachean Ethics,* it is the life in accordance with virtue.[4] Every individual human being seeks happiness; the end of all individual activity is the good. The end or goal of the polis is the common good or the community happiness. Thus, the polis is the highest most inclusive kind of association. It is the association that includes every other kind of human association. It encompasses and embraces and assimilates within its own end the ends of all individuals and all the lesser associations.

Men enter into associations because they are not self-sufficient, because they cannot achieve their own individual happiness without the assistance of others. Individual need or human desire conjoined with individual insufficiency result in associations, cooperative purposive efforts. Again bearing in mind that nature means the completion of a thing and its final excellence, anything necessary to the fulfillment or completion of a thing is also natural to it. Thus air is natural to fire, water to roses, the forest to foxes, migration to geese, and, according to Aristotle, the polis to man. Man is the rational animal; therefore, he is the political animal, the animal who lives in a political association.[5] The full development of speech and reason require political life, and political life, Aristotle observes, is coeval with rules governing behavior. Speech, reason, and political life presuppose each other, are conditions of each other. For language to develop men must interact with enough frequency to assign meanings to sounds. There must be continuity of association so that the meanings can stabilize into a language. The continuity of associations depends upon the existence and enforcement of rules. In every interaction among men, except perhaps the most fleeting, there must be rules, established patterns of conduct, principles of friendly intercourse. Even a band of robbers lives in accordance with rules of behavior, as we acknowledge when we speak of "honor among thieves." Every association of men depends upon the observance of prescribed standards of conduct, in a word, upon politics.

Nature is growth and primarily that into which a thing grows when it is complete. It should be obvious, however, that polises do not grow like roses or oaks. To say that the polis is natural does not mean that men don't have a hand in making cities and political associations. Observation tells us that human action is required, and we are well aware of the act of founding a polity, of drawing up a constitution, of establishing a nation. The polis is natural not because it comes into being totally by itself, for a polis can be constructed. The polis is natural because man is by nature designed to live in one. To say that the polis is natural is to say that men are influenced in the creation of political communities by their own natures. It is to say that living in political communities is as characteristic of men as language. It is to say that a man is designed to live in a political association because he cannot live well, fulfill his rational potential, perfect his being, live the good life outside of one. Thus Aristotle says that the man who lives totally outside of a political community, who has no need of a political community, is either a beast or a god.[6] He is either something lower than man or something higher than man. This does not mean that no one biologists would classify as a member of the species *Homo sapiens* ever lives outside a political association. There are and have been hermits and jungle boys. It means rather that these human beings are like acorns that are not rooted in nourishing soil, that are not planted in their proper environment. They may grow, but they will not grow tall and straight. They will not fulfill their potential, and to that extent are unnatural.

Aristotle demonstrates that the polis is natural to man by tracing its growth out of the elementary associations. The first and most basic association is the union of male and female in the act of procreation.[7] The union of male and female for the continuance of the species is clearly natural. Men may talk of decanting babies from bottles or tell children stories about finding babies under cabbages, and religious beliefs may focus on a virgin birth, but such belong to the realms of the conventional or the sacred, not the natural. The union of male and female for procreation is natural, but it is not exclusively human; plants and animals also associate sexually. This elementary association arises because of the natural insufficiency or the inadequacy of the individual; the individual alone—as individual—cannot reproduce.

The next elementary natural association Aristotle considers is the union of rulers and ruled.[8] While this is a more nearly human association, it is not exclusively so since many animals live in a hierarchical social structure upon which group survival depends. This union of rulers and ruled has as its object the safety of the ruled. To the extent that the authority of the ruler or leader in animal societies is necessary for the preservation of the pack, it is natural. Aristotle concludes that some forms of authority are natural, that ruling and being ruled are not wholly conventional.

The distinction between a natural authority and a conventional authority turns on competence or potential capacity and on common interest. Potential capacity distinguishes a child from what Aristotle calls a natural slave, what we would call a moron, a mentally incompetent person. Both the child and a natural slave are ruled by force because of their incapacity. Persuasion and argument do not suffice to convince a two-year-old that he cannot wander about on the roads, and so he is confined in a playpen, placed in a harness, constantly supervised and not permitted to go where he wills for his own safety. The same is true for morons. The child, however, is potentially competent, and so as he grows, he outgrows the rule of force. As he advances in age and ability, the rule of reason replaces the rule of force until ultimately his own reason is sufficient for his safety, and instead of being ruled by the reason of others, he rules himself and is a man.

Natural slaves do not have potential capacity; they do not grow in reason and so are always ruled by force. This kind of slavery is natural because it is necessary, and it is for the good of the ruled. Conventional slavery, on the other hand, is the forcible rule of the competent. It is not for the good of the ruled, but exclusively for the good of the rulers. It is unnecessary and unnatural. Natural ruling in this sense of authority over incompetent individuals is necessary as essential for continued existence.

Furthermore, ruling is natural on the basis of the common interest of the beings who are not individually self-sufficient although competent. Certain needs can only be satisfied or satisfied at little cost when individuals work together, act in combination. Building bridges and cathedrals, playing baseball, performing Shakespeare, sailing ships, putting out fires, and saving victims of earthquakes, these are group enterprises, and all group activities must be regulated, must be directed and controlled by rules. The rules manage behavior, divide the labor, assign tasks and roles, allot rewards, and define the common benefit. Every group activity is in a sense a form of ruling and being ruled. For every group activity there is a ruler; there is a foreman, an architect, a team manager, a stage director, a captain, a fire chief, a Red Cross director. Ruling is necessary and thus natural. It is indispensable to accomplish a group objective.

The family, the first fully human association, combines these prior elementary associations.[9] It is based on the sexual union of male and female for procreation, on the association of rulers and ruled in the first instance for the safety of the incompetent, children, and in the second for the satisfaction of the needs of the competent, adult members. Even the family is not completely self-sufficient, and so families combine into villages that, through their united efforts, can better provide for food and shelter, engage in trade, and defend territory. Villages in turn combine into a polis, which is the self-sufficient community, the place where all human needs can be satisfied, physical, mental and spiritual, through the united efforts, the aggregated assets, the consolidated achievements of the group. The polis is natural even though men by a deliberate act of the will establish the political community because only in such a community can a man be happy. Only in such a community can a man fulfill his potential.

To possess happiness is to be self-sufficient, but this does not mean a solitary condition, since we know by observation that among the things that a man needs to be happy are friends, family, and fellow citizens. We know by observation and experience that to be lonely, unloved, to be alienated (which means literally to be a stranger, a foreigner, to be set apart, to be a man without a country) are bad conditions, conditions that make for unhappiness. Paradoxically, a man can be self-sufficient only because of the society and cooperation of others. Radical self-reliance, entailing absolute seclusion and total independence of the abilities, resources, and presence of his fellows is not, according to Aristotle, the way of or in the character of man. Even if it is possible for an individual man to live in extreme isolation from his fellows, such a state of being is mere life, not the good life. A dog may walk on two legs, but it does not do it well. Human self-sufficiency and thus human happiness are functions of living in a political community of which the polis is the best model because it is the most inclusive model.

Aristotle's argument for the polis as natural rests primarily on the coincidence of the ends of the individual and the polis, a coincidence that occurs because the specific, natural, and proper human activity, the good life, is attainable only in such a political community. The ultimate end of man is the good life or happiness; the ultimate end of the polis is the common good or the happiness of all the members of the community. The ends of both are in accord, and occur at the same time or place. Thus the polis is natural; men are political animals designed to live in political communities. Any distinction between man and his final community is artificial, abstract, and contrived.

Chapter 4

THE ANCIENTS
The Art of Government

In everything the middle course is best; all things in excess bring
trouble to men.

Plautus

The ancient political philosophers raised the question, Are
political things natural? After a thorough, systematic examination of the issue, they answered, Yes. Since nature as they
understood it was a goal, a final end, this affirmative answer did
not declare all political communities to be equally natural and
hence equally good, but it did confirm the utility and appropriateness of nature as a positive standard by which to evaluate
any particular political community.

If some political associations are more natural than others,
then the most natural political association would be the best
regime simply and would be the model for all other regimes.
Thus the next fundamental question raised by the ancient
philosophers was, What is the best regime simply? This question is a complex one and can be broken down into three more
specific questions. A political association is an association of
rulers and ruled. One obvious subquestion, therefore, is, Who
rules in the best regime simply or what gives title to rule?
Political associations are purposive; they have an end or goal,

and therefore another subquestion is, What are the consequences of such a rule, or what kind of men are produced by this regime? Finally, a political association as a natural thing actualizes itself in time and place, is something that can be. Therefore, the third subquestion is, What are the conditions of this regime, or under what particular circumstances can it exist?

The first task of the political theorist is to search for the best regime simply. If a thing is natural, as politics is according to the ancients, then it has to be discovered or located. The theorist has to look for it rather than invent it. The problem is that every known example is in some way defective, and so the best regime simply must be found in theory. This does not mean, according to Aristotle, that the best regime simply is an impossibility, an imaginary community, a utopia. Rather, it means that though it can be, depending upon accident and circumstance, it is not yet. It is possible, said Aristotle, for the studier, for the wise man who understands the proper function of a thing, to see its final fulfillment prior to its actual occurrence. Thus, a physiologist who thoroughly understood the functions of the human body could have stated the theoretical possibility that a man could run a mile in less than four minutes many years before any human being demonstrated that it could be done in an actual timed race. For years the goal of breaking the four-minute mile was the dream of milers, and many people alive today remember when it was just a theoretical possibility.

Full understanding of the nature of a thing includes a recognition of the necessary conditions of its actualization. For thousands of years men have dreamed of flying to the stars. Once men recognized or discovered the principles or conditions of flight, flying to the stars became a theoretical possibility. Once men developed the necessary equipment, it became a practical possibility. The equipment has been developed. Men have now walked on the moon. They have now landed machines on Mars that allow them to observe and experiment. Within the lifetime of this generation, men may actually walk on Mars. Theory, then, precedes practice and can be actualized given the right equipment or conditions. Theory, in this sense, is a recognition of a conditional possibility.

That a thing is possible does not necessarily mean it is probable. A thing is possible if it may occur, but it is probable if it is more likely to occur than not. Both probability and possibility are functions of chance and/or art. The best regime simply, according to ancient theory, is dependent upon chance, not upon art. As a terminal perfection, it can be actualized only under optimum conditions; such conditions are the exception, out of the ordinary, or rare. Since they are rare, and since they cannot be produced by art, the best regime simply is possible, but not probable. The improbability of the best regime simply in no way detracts from its utility as a standard for political evaluation and political prescription. No man has yet achieved perfect health, which is produced by the combination of perfect heredity and perfect environment. Nonetheless, the concept of health informs both the diagnosis and prescription of the physician. A physician must know what health is, and must recognize conditional possibility in order to prescribe remedies for actual defects. The best regime simply (the healthy regime), a theoretical concept, is the measure for all actual regimes, as the healthy man, a theoretical concept, is the measure of the soundness and vigor in all actual men.

WHO RULES IN THE BEST REGIME SIMPLY?

If political things are natural, title to rule must be based on something natural. Politics is the art of human government or the science of human affairs. Political rule is the rule of men, not the rule of gods or of beasts. Man is a natural being and as such has a terminal excellence. That quality or faculty most specifically human (the human terminal excellence) gives title to rule. Thus, the most natural man, hence, the best man should rule. According to the ancients, the most specifically human faculty is rationality; its highest manifestation is wisdom, hence, the wise rule in the best regime simply.[1]

When title to anything is in question, there are several grounds on which a claim may be made. There may be claims based on discovery, as when an explorer plants his country's flag on a new land. There may be claims based on labor, as when the farmer harvests his crops. There may be claims based on need, as when a hungry man demands a loaf of bread. There may be claims based on simple possession, as when squatters occupy land. There may be claims based on superiority of skill or talent, as when the best violinist calls for the Stradivarius. All of these claims have some legitimate basis. The discoverer, the laborer, the needy, the current possessor, the talented; who has the highest claim? If nature defined as a terminal excellence is your standard, the answer is clear, The man who uses it well, the man who puts it to the best use.

Wisdom is true discernment or right judgment. It is wisdom that permits men to distinguish the just from the unjust, the useful from the harmful, the actual good from the apparent good. It is wisdom that allows men to perceive the natures of things, to judge correctly of possibility and the conditions of possibility. The wise man is the man who will rule well, therefore the wise should rule.

According to the ancient political philosophers, the best regime simply is the regime completely dedicated to the common good, which is the good life or the life in accordance with virtue.[2] This regime is an organic whole in which each of the parts performs its assigned functions in accord with all of the other parts. Thus, the best regime simply is a harmony whose symmetry and balance are unmarred by rebel parts that usurp the function of another part, or by empty parts that do not function at all. The harmony of a great painting such as da Vinci's *Last Supper,* in which each figure, each line, and each color functions to focus our vision on the theme, the head of Christ, is not unlike the harmony of the best regime simply. No rebel spot of bright red in one corner, no blank spots of bare canvas distract our vision of an ordered whole. Since the best regime simply is an organic whole of interrelated, functioning parts, wisdom is title to rule. The expert or the one who possesses the architectonic vision of the harmonious, functioning whole (because he knows the purpose of the whole) is also the one who knows what each part should do.[3] Thus, the expert must have a clear understanding of the universal and the particular. The football coach must understand the game, have a vision of the game as well played. Additionally, he must know what tasks and skills each position, guard, tackle, quarterback, requires. In other words, he knows the duties of each player on the field because he understands the purpose of the game, or he knows how it is well played. He knows what a middle-line-backer must do because he understands the middle-line-backer's duties relative to all of the other positions on the field. He can pick the particularly appropriate man to fill the middle-line-backer's position because he knows what skills and talents are required for the position, and because he can recognize those skills and talents in individuals. Someone must direct or order the parts, someone must assign each part to its *proper* place, and this can only be the wise man, the man who judges correctly, who sees truly, who can distinguish the real good from the apparent good, the useful from the useless, the appropriate from the inappropriate.

The most famous and enduring analogy to the best regime simply is the ship of state, used by Socrates to illustrate the predominant claim of the wise to rule.[4] The ship of state is an excellent analogy because a ship is an easily recognized functioning whole. Its dedication to the common good of all aboard as literally their lifeboat illustrates the dependence or subordinance of all the parts to the whole. Finally, the command or rule of the expert, of the pilot, who knows the waters and who can set a true course, is patently necessary to the survival of the ship.

In the best regime simply the wise man is king, not constitutional monarch; or, in this regime, wisdom rules unhampered, unrestrained, and unlimited. No law, no rule, no regulation can logically bind true knowledge.[5] Lest this classical understanding offend our modern sensibilities, consider that in the heaven of the Judeo-Christian tradition, God, who is omniscient, all-knowing, rules absolutely—there are no elections, no referendums, and no recall in heaven. Heaven is a kingdom, not a democratic republic. Law as a general rule or principle is a kind of frozen wisdom. It is rigid, static, blind to particularity; but, the wise man has the advantage over the frozen wisdom of the law because he can be flexible, dynamic, and can perceive particularity. The best regime simply is the regime completely dedicated to the common good, the good of all, which is the happiness of all, and it is ruled absolutely by the wise man who knows the true purpose or terminal excellence of man and who recognizes the potential of each. Wisdom is the highest title to rule.

WHAT ARE THE CONSEQUENCES OF THIS RULE?

Nature is not merely a characteristic way, but also a final excellence, and the characteristic way of man, which is speech and reason, has a final excellence—the life in accordance with virtue. Virtue is the health of the soul. If the wise man, the man who can distinguish the real good from the apparent good, rules, the regime can produce men with healthy souls or it can educate each man to that degree and variety of virtue for which he has potential. It can produce men who are courageous, men who are moderate, men who are just, men who are wise. The wise ruler, said Socrates, is like an expert horse trainer who recognizes the individual particular capacities of each and devises an appropriate training program for all.[6] The best regime simply is dedicated to human excellence and educates men to the virtues. The test of any regime is the kind of men it produces, and the best regime simply is designed to produce good men.

In this regime and in this regime only, the good man can be identical with the good citizen.[7] This identity is the essence of the best regime simply. The good man who is a good citizen is the concrete resolution of one of the most fundamental and intransigent problems of human life—the conflict of law and justice. Outside of the best regime simply, the virtues of the good man and the good citizen differ. According to Aristotle's definition, a citizen is a ruler and an office holder.[8] A citizen participates in the offices of judging (usually as a juror) and legislating (usually by voting). Each regime decides who may and who may not perform these offices, who is and who is not a citizen. In all regimes, there are qualifications for the office of citizen. Residence of itself does not make one a citizen, since all regimes exclude resident aliens and slaves from the office. Some societies have age, or wealth, or class, or religious qualifications for the office of citizen. Just as not everyone is a citizen, not everyone is a good citizen. A good citizen is loyal to his country and performs his assigned role well. But a good citizen is not necessarily a good man. A good man is just; a good citizen is law-abiding. In fact, since a regime may be good or bad, just or unjust, the good citizen may even be a bad man. In Nazi Germany, a man could have been a good citizen, but, given the character of his regime, such a citizen could not have been a good man.

Further, since there are many different regimes, there are many different types of good citizens or many forms of civic excellence.[9] By very rough analogy, there are many different sports each requiring different athletic skills, or different combinations of athletic skills. A good football player is not necessarily a good swimmer. A good basketball player is not necessarily a good gymnast. We say a man is a good athlete, and yet we most frequently focus on his performance in a particular, distinct sport. Despite this, the concept of the good athlete simply, the man with skills applicable to all cases, remains, if only because observation tells us that one sport emphasizes or exaggerates certain skills at the expense of others. Who is the complete athlete? Who has the cardinal athletic virtues? Questions like these are behind events such as the decathlon, which seeks to discover which man excels at ten different track and field events. The decathlon champion, not the winner of a single specialized event, is often considered to be the complete, the universal athlete.

The good citizen, as Aristotle pointed out, is relative to his regime, because the good citizen is the law-abiding citizen, and the laws of each regime are particular, and pertain to that specific time and place. The good man, however, is a universal; he is always and everywhere the same; he is everywhere the man who possesses the cardinal virtues. In all other regimes, there will be a tension between the good man and the good citizen because in all other regimes there is some conflict between justice, which is a universal, and law, which is particular. The tension between justice and law disappears when the wise man rules.

Since a regime is made up of citizens who associate to pool their talents for their mutual benefit, the ruler must judge correctly what their individual natures are, or he must understand what each member of the whole can do well, thereby to place him in the proper job and educate him to the appropriate virtues. On the ship of state, men are assigned different tasks: one pulls the oars, another sets the sails, and another takes the helm. If the wise man who knows the natures of men rules, then neither the Peter Principle, wherein a man rises to his level of incompetence, nor what we might term the "Paul" Principle, wherein a man fails to rise to the full level of his competence, will obtain. Not all men will achieve the highest excellence, because men have differing talents and the full achievement of one will differ from the full achievement of another. The ancients were not egalitarians.[10] Only a rare few men have the potential to achieve the terminal excellence. But all will be educated to the level of excellence of which they are capable, and all will be functioning parts of a whole dedicated to human excellence.

The best regime simply, therefore, will not be egalitarian in the modern sense of the simple equality of all citizens or of the equal natural rights of men, because when nature, defined as a terminal excellence, is your standard, simple equality is manifestly unjust.[11] We know by observation that some men are taller, or stronger, or faster, or smarter, or more energetic, or more virtuous than others. Equalization of reward may hurt the talented and the industrious, thereby encouraging sloth and mediocrity rather than exertion and excellence. If it were decreed (which most instructors will hasten to assure you it is not) that every student in a political theory course had an equal property right to an A+, the decree could be considered in two lights: it could be considered extremely generous, and generosity is a virtue; but it could also be considered unjust, unfair to those who worked hard and achieved a high degree of competence in the subject matter.

In addition to being unjust, equality in all things may be impolitic and imprudent. Consider that if men are in fact simply equal, they are equally capable of performing the offices of government. A truly egalitarian regime would select its presidents, its governors and its mayors by lot. To the extent that we are unwilling to adopt such a method of selecting our leaders, we are not simple egalitarians. We apparently are unwilling to use such a method; we vote for our leaders. In voting for a leader, we are implicitly saying that in our judgment one man is *better* qualified than another. We are saying that in our judgment the candidates are not equal. Equality may be a noble ideal, but one can have too much of a good thing, as too much wine.

In political associations, men pool their talents for their mutual benefit, which is the common good, but because of their different capacities, they make different contributions to the common good—contributions that differ in both quantity and quality. Furthermore, in all actual political associations, circumstances have an effect on the value of contributions to the common good. In time of famine, the valuable man is the farmer; in time of disease, the valuable man is the physician. This point is charmingly illustrated in a little known work of L. Frank Baum, author of the *Wizard of Oz*. In a lovely bit of political satire, he tells of an army made up of generals, colonels, majors, and one private, a man named Files. With a surplus of decision-makers and a scarcity of fighters, the contribution of Private Files appreciates, and he becomes the most valuable man. We can't all be generals, but if we could, generals would not be esteemed or influential.

Aristotle, ever practical, does take circumstance into consideration, as we shall see in his advice to prospective founders. Nevertheless, he points out that the true, the proper conception of justice is based on the end for which the state exists, namely the good life. Thus, he corrects both the democrat and the oligarch for their partial conceptions of justice:

> In democracies, for example, justice is considered to mean equality. It does mean equality—but equality for those who are equal, and not for all. In oligarchies, again, inequality in the distribution of office is considered to be just; and indeed it is—but only for those who are unequal, and not for all.[12]

The best regime simply will be a meritocracy where each receives from the regime according to what is good for him and thus for the regime itself.[13] All rewards or rights in this regime are a product of performance or of duties. Since the level of performance is determined and limited by the specific abilities of the individual, inequality of reward, or reward according to merit, is neither arbitrary nor capricious but rather is simply just as each receives what he deserves. The principle of this regime is from each according to his ability, to each according to his contribution.[14] Rights and duties are reciprocal in the regime dedicated to human excellence.

WHAT ARE THE NECESSARY CONDITIONS OF THE BEST REGIME SIMPLY?

If the best regime simply is a possible regime, we must consider under what conditions it could be actualized. The first condition is, obviously, the existence of the natural ruler. There must be, at a given time and place, a wise man, one who in fact possesses the necessary expertise. Secondly, he must become the ruler. His assumption of the position turns on his willingness to rule and/or on the willingness of the many who are not wise to be ruled by him. Thus, the condition of the best regime simply is the coincidence of wisdom and consent.

This being the case, the best regime simply may be possible, but it is not very probable. Truly wise men are rarely among us. When they are (and let us assume for the sake of argument that Socrates was one such) they do not want to rule.[15] Ruling as it is done in the best regime is a burden; it is for the benefit of the ruled, not for the benefit of the ruler. The wise man will not consent to be the ruler because it is a full time job, and while it is the job that only he can do well, it is not the only job he can do well, nor is it the job that will perfect his own soul. The good life is not the life of self-sacrifice but of self-fulfillment.

The whole is always greater than its parts, and the whole that philosophers call the Good or the ordered cosmos is always beyond. There is always more to know. The wise man loves wisdom, and wisdom is not the same thing as benevolence. To accept the burden of ruling would take time away from the pursuit of knowledge. The proper task of the philosopher and his own individual good, the philosophic life, are not necessarily compatible with the common good. Actualization of the best regime requires the use and abuse of the best of men. The wise man not only will not volunteer, he must be compelled to rule.

Even if a wise man were benevolent enough to volunteer to rule, he could not force the many less wise to obey him. Consent of the ruled, consent of the many, is thus a necessary though not a sufficient condition of the best regime simply.[16]

Since the many are not wise themselves, they are not likely to recognize his wisdom and to accept his rule or to compel him to rule. The rule of the wise, then, can come to pass as a mere matter of the chance selection of the wise by the unwise. It is a possible regime because the unwise can select a wise man and compel him to be the ruler, but it is improbable because it depends upon the coincidence of two rare events, the chance appearance of the truly wise man and his chance selection by the many unwise.

The conditions necessary for the actualization of the best regime simply are not only rarely present, but are beyond the control of men. As expert athletic analysts speculate on the possibility of a new world record in a 1500-meter race, they will take note of the wind, the altitude, the humidity, the possibility of rain, the health of the leading contestants, their relative starting positions, and their past performances. Even if all of these factors appear to be favorable, there is always the luck of the race—someone may fall or be bumped and a new record will not be set. What can be achieved in any given set of particular circumstances is not the same thing as what can be achieved as a theoretical possibility where all the most favorable circumstances coincide.

The answers to our questions regarding the best regime simply are clear. Who rules in this regime? The wise rule with the consent of the many, or wisdom plus consent are title to rule. What are the consequences of such rule? The common good or the life in accordance with virtue. Under what particular circumstances can this regime be actualized? Conditions controlled by chance. The best regime simply is possible, but it is not probable. Politics is, however, a practical art, and as such must provide advice for ordinary regimes, must be applicable to use in ordinary matters. So, in addition to the discovery of the best regime simply, the political scientist must also be concerned with the discovery of the best practical regime, that is, the best under ordinary circumstances. The best practical regime is discovered by assessing the particular circumstances at hand, and comparing them to the circumstances necessary for the best regime simply. Knowledge of the best regime simply is necessarily prior to discovery of the best practical regime.

The fact that there is a best regime simply, and that it is known merely as a theoretical possibility does not make all other regimes illegitimate. If wisdom is title to rule, and wisdom is true judgment or right discernment, then the actually wise man, as opposed to the daydreamer, sees truly the particular circumstances that obtain in a given time and place, and he judges correctly as to what level of political achievement is possible at that specific time and in that specific place. The wise man knows the nature and limits of politics. What can be done is a function of expert knowledge plus the equipment provided to the expert. A master engineer who understands the nature of bridges may have drawn the blueprints for a magnificent bridge, but in order to construct that bridge, he must have steel. If he does not have steel, if he has only stone or wood at his disposal, he will change the design of his bridge since the kind of material he must work with limits bridge-building possibility. The bridge he builds out of stone will look quite different from the bridge he builds out of wood or steel. His claim to expertise rests on his understanding of the whole of the bridge-builder's art. He is an expert because he knows how to build many different kinds of bridges, and this because he understands the nature of bridges and the natures and thus the limits of various kinds of materials. When options are limited, the stone bridge is as much a bridge, as legitimate a bridge, as the steel one. And, if the engineer prefers the steel bridge as superior in some way or another, he does not, when faced with circumstances where steel is not available, sit idly lamenting that he cannot build the ideal bridge, but rather, knowing that a bridge is desired or needed, builds the best bridge possible given the equipment available to him. The best practical regime must be a compromise between expertise, knowledge of the good for man as man, and material, the particular capacities and limitations of the men of a given historical time and place.

The political scientist, as a practitioner of a practical art, must be able to see the universal in the particular. His ability to distinguish what is temporal from what is timeless will allow him to accommodate and apply his expertise to the circumstances as they are. Just as the master engineer can design a great variety of bridges, each design adapted to the specific site, so a master of the art of politics can design a regime suitable for a particular people. Further, every bridge design, no matter what its specific appearance, is controlled or directed by the end or purpose of bridges—to afford safe passage. The goodness or value of the design is determined by its fulfillment of the end or goal. A bridge that does not allow safe passage is not a good bridge, however sturdy and strong it may appear, and a regime that is not directed toward the common good is not a good regime.

Although each bridge is somewhat unique, there are basic or primary designs, and likewise basic forms of government. Among the basic or primary designs is one that is most practicable, that is appropriate or suitable in most circumstances. This design is the most usable design and requires only minor alterations before it can be implemented. Aristotle calls this basic design the best practical regime.

WHO RULES IN THE BEST PRACTICAL REGIME?

Aristotle, who may claim to be the first political scientist, begins his search for the best practical regime by examining and classifying actual regimes. His analysis is guided by the principle that the true goal and proper end of ruling is the common good. Regimes are, then, classified by the consequences of the rule. Good regimes pursue the common good, and bad regimes pursue some private good. In the actual world, this proper goal of regimes can be sought or approximated by several different designs, just as safe passage can be achieved by a steel, or a stone, or a wood bridge. Therefore, Aristotle considers the alternatives and argues that there are three basic designs that can achieve the end: the rule of one, the rule of the few, and the rule of the many. This exhausts the alternatives since the rule of all is the same thing as the rule of none, anarchy. (If everyone is ruling, no one is being ruled and so there is no government.) The classification scheme drawn under these principles is the following:[17]

	Common Good	Private Good
one	kingship	tyranny
few	aristocracy	oligarchy
many	polity	democracy

Number, however, is only an incidental and not an essential or distinctive factor in ruling.[18] As Aristotle is quick to point out, the rich are almost always and everywhere the few, and the poor are almost always and everywhere the many. Recognition of the fact that number is accidental leads Aristotle to reexamine the question of who rules in order to introduce qualitative considerations. Again the goal of the regime, the common good, serves as the guiding principle.

There are, according to Aristotle five differing contenders for the title of ruler: the people, the rich, the few talented, the one best, and the tyrant.[19] Each of the contenders claims to have something to contribute to the common good: the people their numbers or strength, the rich their money, the few talented their skills, the one best his virtue, and the tyrant his power or strength. Although there are five claimants, Aristotle takes seriously the claims of only two: the one best and the people.[20] There may be five claimants, but there are only three core contributions to political life, three basic ingredients of a viable regime: virtue, wealth, and numbers. The claim of the few talented is merely a variation of or the diverse manifestation of virtue. The claim of the tyrant, superior power or strength, is a factor of numbers or money. More to the point, there may be three core contributions, but there are only two factors in the true goal of political life: the good and the common. The one best most closely approximates the first factor, and the people most closely approximate the second factor. (Wealth may be a core contribution, but, unlike the other two, is merely a means and is not an element of the final goal.) Since Aristotle's standard is the end, it follows that those two claimants who prefigure the end would be taken most seriously.

If each contribution is an actual contribution, that is if each is a necessary factor, a useful addition to the common end, then justice (which is distributive) requires these claims be reconciled. The political art, the art of ruling, is the art of compromise, of adjustment, of harmony, and thus of reconciliation.

Interestingly, the claim of the people is the most clearly political of the five claims because it is based on collective qualities or the association and combination of individual qualities. This being the case, the people can make the same kinds of contributions as all of the other claimants.[21] The collective strength or power of the people can match or indeed surpass that of the tyrant; their collective wealth can match or surpass the wealth of the rich; their collective skills can match or surpass the skills of the few talented; and their collective wisdom can, in the form of practical wisdom, that derived from experience, match the wisdom of the one best.

The people have a serious and substantial claim to the title of ruler. Their title to rule, however, rests on the probability that they can in fact collectively make all of these contributions, or that the claims of all can be harmonized in the people. It is possible that one man or a few may have more wealth than the collective wealth of the many, or that a few are stronger than the collective strength of the many, or that a few are more talented than the collective talents of the many.[22] In such cases political harmony is jeopardized. Extreme disproportion of contribution destroys political associations. The whole to be a whole must always be greater than any of its parts. When one of the parts is so prominent and conspicuous, that is, it extends beyond its proper function and usurps the functions of the other parts, then the whole is disordered and destroyed. Such a part is like a cancerous cell in the body, which grows and multiplies beyond its assigned place, and in so doing consumes the space and thus the functions of the other parts.

The remedy to the disproportion or disorder of the body politic is the same as the remedy for cancer: excision, or, in its political form, ostracism.[23] This is politically just (just from the perspective of the whole, or from the necessities of association, though not perhaps simply just) with regard to every disproportion but one. The exception to the principle of ostracism is, of course, preeminent virtue. To cast out the best man would be unjust simply and unjust politically. The best, the most virtuous man must be king. Virtuous men are the goal of the regime; thus it is politically unjust, not to mention contradictory, to cast out such men. To subject the most virtuous man to the rule of the less virtuous would be unnatural, subordinating the superior to the inferior. Further, the virtuous man has the only sufficient title to rule. All of the other contributors are incapable of final accomplishment. The common good, which is the goal of the regime, cannot be fully achieved unless the wise man simply rules. The contributions of all the other claimants, even when ordered and harmonized, can only approximate or approach the common good.

The case for an absolute kingship, however, rests on the actual preeminence in virtue of one man. Since this is a very rare occurrence, Aristotle maintains that in general practice it is better to be ruled by law, that is a constitutional monarchy, aristocracy, or polity, than by the unfettered personal rule of the best man.[24] The case for the rule of law is impartiality. Law can be more rational and dispassionate than man. The case for personal rule unfettered by law is flexibility and recognition of special circumstance. Personal rule can give greater consideration to the unique, the particular than can law. On balance, Aristotle concludes that the rule of law is preferable to the personal rule of men since all men have limitations, since personal rule inevitably faces the problem of succession, and since even an absolute ruler must be guided by general principles which he adapts to the specific circumstances.

The rule of the wise man is, as has already been demonstrated, impractical and improbable. In theory the wise man should rule absolutely, but in practice it is difficult to see who the wise are. It is easier to see who the many are. Furthermore, the consent of the many must be obtained if the regime is to be viable. Aristotle, always conscious of the limits of theory, concludes that the people must rule in the best practical regime.[25] Facility of identification coupled with ease in obtaining consent make the rule of the people the most practical alternative.

The problem with the rule of the people is how it can be directed toward the common good—how it can serve its proper purpose. As Aristotle perceives it, the problem is one of reconciling the two most prevalent contributions, wealth and numbers. The answer is a large middle class.[26] The middle class is made up of the poorer of the rich and the richer of the poor. The middle class is a blend or harmony of the democratic principle of numbers and the oligarchic principle of wealth. The better the blend the more likely democrats will mistake it for democracy and oligarchs will mistake it for oligarchy. Who, then, rules in the best practical regime? The people and specifically the middle class.

Polity, the name Aristotle gives to the good rule of the many, is the best practical regime. It is a mixed regime, combining the principles of oligarchy and democracy; it is the rule of the middle class. The middle class is a mean and not a mediocrity, for, as Aristotle points out in *The Nicomachean Ethics,* goodness lies in the mean between two extremes, as courage is a mean between rashness and cowardice.[27] In his famous praise of the middle class, Aristotle observes that the middle class possesses two virtues in addition to the collective wisdom already discovered in the people.[28] First, men of the middle class are moderate; they will listen to reason. The rich are arrogant and contemptuous. The poor are envious and mean spirited. The middle class does not covet the goods of others, and others do not covet their goods. Second, they are courageous for they are the arms-bearing class.

WHAT ARE THE CONSEQUENCES OF THIS RULE?

Although the middle class can base its claim to rule on three virtues: collective wisdom, courage, and moderation, it is the last virtue that is most significant because moderation is *the* political virtue, the harmonizing virtue. To be moderate is to keep within reasonable limits, to avoid excess and extremes. The moderation of the middle class is a function of its position as the midpoint on the line of poverty and wealth, a position that makes it a compromise or balance between the two opposing economic classes. Thus, the rule of the middle class can provide an economic equilibrium that produces political stability. The moderation of the middle class tempers the extreme claims of the rich and the poor; it restrains their mutual hostilities; it cushions economic class conflict; it reduces political polarization; it limits the rise of faction. The moderate middle class bridges the chasm that divides and isolates the rich and the poor. Because the middle class is moderate, its rule will be milder, less burdensome than the rule of either the democrats or the oligarchs. Since the middle class is a mean, it is in a better position to understand and sympathize with the desires of both the democrats and the oligarchs. The interest of the middle class, therefore, is closer to the common interest than the interests of either of the polar extremes.

The middle class is, further, everybody's second choice as ruler. Both the rich and the poor would prefer their own class to rule, but if denied their own domination, each would, as the next best thing, prefer the rule of the middle class. The rich would rather be ruled by the middle class than by the poor for they trust the sober middle class will not expropriate property.

The poor would rather be ruled by the middle class than by the rich for they trust the temperate middle class will not be oppressive.

Aristotle makes much of the fact that a polity ruled by a large middle class is the most faction-free of the forms of government.[29] Faction, the pursuit of private group or class interest, is the disease of constitutions, the source of their destruction. Because the interest of the middle class combines and unites the interests of the democratic and oligarchic factions, because the middle class is each faction's second choice as ruling class, it will command a solid and general allegiance. The rule of the middle class is, Aristotle argues, the most stable of all the practical regimes.

Stability is a very high political value, but it is not the highest, and it is not the ultimate justification for the rule of the middle class. That justification lies in its resistance to tyranny. Tyranny combines the worst perversions of oligarchy and democracy since it is at once arrogant and mean spirited, oppressive and envious, seeking both to amass wealth and to destroy all preeminent men. Tyranny is least likely to emerge out of a middle class polity, the polity that consciously and unconsciously avoids all extremes.[30] This, perhaps, is Aristotle's greatest praise of the rule of the middle class, that its least likely consequence is tyranny. What are the consequences of the rule of the middle class? Moderation, stability and above all else relative immunity to the most devastating of all political diseases—tyranny.

What Regime is Appropriate Under What Conditions?

Aristotle's advice to a prospective founder is: Whenever there is a large middle class, institute a polity, because this form reconciles the basic contributions to political life—virtue, wealth, and numbers. Since, however, a large middle class is a necessary condition of the best practical regime, and since there often is not a large middle class, Aristotle must consider which form of government is most suitable to a variety of different circumstances. Even the best practical regime is not appropriate for all men in all places and times.

Again, drawing on the idea that politics is the art of compromise and of reconciliation of essentially different civic contributions, Aristotle establishes the principle that a regime must be formed around the strongest element of the people.[31] The prospective founder, then, must closely observe the people and must weigh the relative contributions of each class. Once he discovers the strongest element, he must base the regime on that element. If he does not, he is engaged in a futile effort. The form or design will be incompatible with the material, the structure will be defective and will soon be destroyed by the elemental force among the people. Therefore, if a founder discovers that the poor are the strongest element, that the numbers of the poor outweigh the wealth of the rich, he must institute a democracy. If the wealth of the few outweighs the numbers of the poor, then he must institute an oligarchy. Oligarchy and democracy are classified among the bad regimes. Nonetheless, a wise founder will select those forms whenever the circumstances dictate. Wisdom recognizes necessity, and politics is the art of the best possible, not of the best simply.

Chapter 5

THE MODERNS

The Alteration of the Standard

Everyman is the architect of his own fortune.

Sallust

The modern political philosophers no less than the ancient took their bearings about things political from the concept of nature. Their understanding of nature, however, differed sufficiently from that of the ancients to produce a new and antithetical answer to the fundamental question, Are political things natural? Their answer was, No, political things are not natural, they are artificial and conventional; they are simply manmade.

The moderns' evaluation of political things differed from that of the ancients because although the standard for measurement continued to be a concept of nature, the meaning of nature underwent a radical revision, a revision that marks the beginning of modernity. Modern political thought begins in the sixteenth century with Niccolo Machiavelli. Machiavelli has a bad reputation among laymen, and his claim to be the founder of modern political thought is, therefore, often neglected. Furthermore, Machiavelli does not explicitly and directly challenge the ancient teaching on nature. For all his shocking frankness about political things, his new thesis (antithesis) about nature is implicit in what appears to be a "how to do it" book for aspiring rulers.[1]

The ancients had defined nature as the fundamental way or character of a thing in its final fulfillment, the way it seeks to be. For Machiavelli, nature is merely the way things are. It is not a guide and a goal; it is a place to begin, an occasion for action. The way things are, according to the ancients, is in almost all particular instances defective, imperfect, and unfinished. The way things are, therefore, is not completely natural and not a proper or useful standard for imitation, emulation, or evaluation. Nevertheless, Machiavelli contends that the way things are, rather than the way they ought to be, is the more proper subject matter of political science.[2] Since Machiavelli agrees with the ancients that the way things are is not happy, harmonious, or well ordered, nature—the way things are—is not and cannot be a model to be imitated or a goal to be achieved.[3] Instead, nature is something to be overcome.

Machiavelli revises and reduces the concept of nature precisely because he fully agrees with the ancients that the proper political goal is the *common* good and precisely because he fully agrees with the ancients that the role of the political philosopher is to consider what political men ought to do.[4] His quarrel with the ancients is not that they adopted nature as their gauge, but rather that they took their bearings from what is *uncommon* in man, the perception that happiness lies in virtue, and from what is uncommon in the human condition, fortunate circumstances.[5]

A very few men are philosophers, saints, or heroes. Philosophers, saints, and heroes are to be admired and (one would hope) to be emulated, but to assume that most men are philosophers, saints, or heroes and to act on that assumption is, according to Machiavelli, to seek someone's ruin, most likely one's own.[6] Thus Machiavelli challenged the propriety, the appropriateness of a standard achievable only by the very few. To be appropriate the standard, he said, must take account of human fraility. A philosopher will be just without law, a saint will bear the burdens of others, a hero will risk his life, but the ordinary man, the average man, you and I, will not.

The term natural denotes conformity to what is expected. But, what is expected may be, on the one hand, what is probable, typical, or usual (as in we expect the children will be hungry after school) and on the other hand, what is right, proper, or virtuous (as in we expect the best of our students). The problem is that what is virtuous or excellent is not what is usual. As these two denotations are different, they appear to call for different standards, or at least a rather flexible standard.

In the sports world, a flexible standard is created by establishing leagues or divisions based on size, skill, and past performance or by seeding the competitors. One does not pit Notre Dame against Slippery Rock State College in football. One does not schedule the lightweight champion against the heavyweight champion in boxing. In tennis tournaments, the players are seeded so that the more skilled competitors meet only in the later events. In golf, matches between professionals and amateurs are handicapped, the better players must give strokes to the amateurs. These divisions, seedings, and handicaps are created so that those who cannot meet the highest mark will not be so discouraged that they will give up or be defeated far short of what they can achieve. Machiavelli appears to be saying that if politics is to be directed toward the common good, it cannot seek to be in the heroic league, that distinguished by true excellence. It cannot be in the major league, the league in which no handicaps are given, no allowances made, the league in which each contestant is held to the highest standard. Politics, he suggests, must be in the prosaic league, that characterized by ordinary merit. It must be in the minor league, the league where adjustments are made and accommodations are given, the league in which contestants are held to a flexible standard.

The ancients, as Machiavelli knew, were very much aware of the human penchant to mistake the apparent good for the real good, and they were fully aware of the opposition between nature as a terminal excellence and chance. They knew that while everything noble is just, not everything just is noble, as punishment for crime may be just but surely is not noble. They knew that there are not only times that try men's souls, but also circumstances that transpose what is praiseworthy and blameworthy, as the soldier-guardians of Socrates' city were to be like watchdogs—gentle with friends, harsh with strangers.[7] They knew what men ought to do in war differs from what they ought to do in peace. They knew, and yet they were largely silent about these things in their political prescriptions, perhaps because they believed it unnecessary to teach such things, or perhaps because they would not give necessity the praise of virtue.

Although Aristotle discusses at length what regime is most practicable under what specific conditions, and although he advises potential founders that they must even settle for theoretically bad regimes, such as democracy or oligarchy, when the material and/or the circumstances dictate, he, nonetheless, always takes his bearings from the highest possibility for man.[8] Although Socrates advised Crito to be law-abiding, to be loyal to the regime that condemned a philosopher, Socrates too always took his bearings from the highest possibility for man.[9] These two philosophers lacked neither flexibility nor common sense, but they refused to be guided by mere life, they looked to the good life. Lest we too contemptuously reject Machiavelli's critique of the ancients' position, let us recall that mere life is the absolute precondition, the *sine qua non,* of the good life. On returning to work after recovering from a heart attack, a former colleague of mine (one who yielded to none in his admiration of Aristotle) once said to me, "Aristotle was wrong, mere life is more important than the good life."

Machiavelli's quarrel with the ancients is that their political prescriptions are guided by the highest potential of a few in unusual circumstances. The virtuous life is not the common good because virtue is too high a goal. Peace and prosperity are the common good. The ancients, he says, expect too much and a rigid adherence to their standard results in ruin, the loss of what the common man really wants—peace and prosperity.[10] If nature as a terminal excellence is an unreal standard, and nature as the way things are is neither happy, harmonious, nor well ordered, then the political art is not to emulate, or imitate nature, but to improve upon it, to transcend it. Thus, the province of nature is contracted and the province of art or convention is expanded.

Machiavelli does not discuss nature per se, and therefore this point may be easily missed. Disregarding the classical terminology, which focuses on the opposition between nature and convention, Machiavelli substitutes the opposition between virtue and fortune. Virtue, as traditionally understood, was a subset or subclassification (though the highest ranking subset) of the more general and inclusive class—traits, features, capacities, dispositions, and powers. The virtues were those traits, features, capacities, and powers that were admirable, excellent, noble, or good, while the vices were those that were reprehensible, base, or evil. Machiavelli expands the term virtue so that it includes all of those traits, features, capacities, and powers that are normally called vices.[11] For Machiavelli, virtue is a morally neutral term. As he expands the term, virtue does not mean moral rectitude or moral excellence, but rather sheer ability, skill, technical or artistic mastery, talent, or power.

The exercise of virtue in this new sense is the *process* by which artifacts and conventions are created. It is the efficient cause of the artificial, as carpentry is the skill that causes or converts a natural object, oak, into an artifact, a chair. Virtue is human work or endeavor as contrasted with nature, that which is, without human effort. Virtue, as Machiavelli has redefined it, sounds very similar to the ancient concept of art, the antonym of nature. Ironically, the term Machiavelli chooses to replace the ancient term, art, is the very term the ancients most closely associate with nature, virtue. According to the ancients, virtue is a terminal excellence, and it is the specific happiness of men. Therefore, the ancients held that virtue and nature are identical in men; the virtuous man is the man who has fulfilled his potential; the most natural man, the happiest man is the most virtuous man.

Fortune, on the other hand, is merely that which happens, whatever is there; it is the elements of the situation as they present themselves to the potential artisan.[12] Fortune sounds very similar to the ancient concept of nature in its priority to art, in its status as a given or condition of man's activity. In the 25th chapter of *The Prince,* Machiavelli appears to reinforce the similarity between fortune and nature by comparing fortune to such natural phenomena as a storm, a river, and finally a woman.[13] However, fortune is not the same thing as the classical conception of nature. Fortune is whatever happens whether good or bad, but the classical conception of nature is a positive one—the virtue or perfection of the thing, and so limited to the good. Machiavelli makes no distinction between Dame Fortune and her daughter Miss Fortune. Additionally, fortune is chance —random, variable, aimless, unknown, and unknowable. But, the classical concept of nature is of an ordered purposive whole of which each part is essential, indispensible, proportionate, and which, because it is ordered and purposive, is knowable.

The very metaphors for fortune that Machiavelli chooses draw our attention to the fundamental chaos of the conditions within which human life occurs. A storm is a disturbance, a great whirling motion, violent and destructive. The river Machiavelli chooses for his comparison is wild and turbulent, again disturbed, full of motion and a violent force. Finally, Machiavelli compares fortune not just to a woman but to a capricious and fickle woman. All of the metaphors share the idea of confused change, of unintelligible mysterious motion, and of destructiveness.

Fortune is not simply a new term for nature, it is a reduction of and replacement for nature. Just as Machiavelli expands and changes the classical conception of virtue, he reduces and thus changes the classical conception of nature. The opposition Machiavelli gives us is, then, a radically new opposition, a distinction in which independent human activity (virtue) is a potential counterforce that overcomes or masters whatever happens, whatever is there (fortune). It is a distinction in which man, the potential creator of order, confronts and must overcome a fundamental disorder.

There are many reasons why Machiavelli chose to change the terms in dealing with this fundamental distinction between nature and convention, but one primary purpose was to allow us to see the distinction in an entirely new way, a way in which art is not a mere secondary phenomenon, a reflection and imitation of nature, the primary phenomenon. In defining nature as the truest and best manifestation, the ancients focused our vision on the end, taught us to aspire toward fulfillment, clarified our goals, and provided a standard to measure achievement. Machiavelli's reduction of nature to that which is, or the way we find things to be, turns us completely about so that we perceive nature as a beginning not an end, a starting place not a stopping point, an opportunity not an achievement, an opening not a limitation. The ancients have us look at nature as a target or a finish line that we may be able to answer the questions, What is the purpose of human life? What are we for? What can we become? How close are we to the goal? Machiavelli has us look at nature as the starting line or springboard that we may ask, What can we do now? How can we change these things? What are the powers of human beings? How far have we gone?

For the ancients, nature is ahead of us; it is where we are going. For Machiavelli, nature is behind us; it is what we are leaving. We leave nature behind as we exercise our virtue, our abilities and our faculties, to overcome what is—fortune. If fortune is a wild natural force like a storm, a river, or a fickle woman, then fortune can be tamed, nature can be overcome. Rivers can be dammed, men can build shelters against the storms, and a bold lover can capture the fancy of a fickle woman. Nature, according to the ancients, is that which is not controlled by man, but Machiavelli teaches that fortune, which he said controls half the affairs of men, can be overcome by a man who is virtuous—able and adaptable.[14] The classical understanding of nature as a limitation on being began to disappear as Machiavelli launched a new concept of nature that served as the basis of modern thought.

So modernity begins with the revision of the concept of nature. To the ancients nature meant growth, gradual development, a process of becoming that seeks being. Nature is a kind of motion, but it is ordered and purposive motion, a motion that can be understood and deciphered from a point of rest that is the completion and fulfillment of motion, as a horserace becomes intelligible when we know where the finish line is. The moderns rejected limited and purposive growth as the definitive characteristic of nature. They see little or no design, no pattern, no intentionality in the motion they called nature. Nature is merely wild motion, aimless, designless, improvident, undirected causation. It is chance, what we find at the primitive beginning. The modern theory of nature is like a poker game where significance or value is to be found in the betting (control of being) and bluffing (changing being) rather than in the cards themselves, what one is dealt. The ancient theory of nature is more like a bridge game where significance and value are to be found in the bidding (recognition of potential being) and in the play (fulfillment of being) or making the most of what one is dealt.

Nature becomes the beginning point rather than the end; nature becomes what is rather than what is excellent; nature becomes opportunity rather than limitation. All that was retained of the classical conception of nature after Machiavelli had turned it upside down was that nature was the way of a thing that was not made by man.

The importance of Machiavelli's new teaching on nature, a teaching that attempts to destroy the concept of nature as a limitation on being, is enormous. Machiavelli claimed that it would liberate men from the prison of an unreal existence, what he called imaginary republics, and return them to the earth. But the earth to which Machiavelli returned men was a fundamentally different earth, an earth whose finiteness was questionable, whose possibilities were endless. And, the men that Machiavelli would bring back to earth were a new breed of men, men who no longer perceived themselves as a part, if a superior and dominant part, of an ordered whole. Rather, this new breed of men perceived themselves as demi-gods who though in the whole were not necessarily of it because they could by an act of will change and control the parts and perhaps even the whole itself.

Nature, as the ancients understood it, was an independent order of things, distinct from the order created by men (art and convention) and distinct as well from the order created by the gods, the sacred and the miraculous. The ancients understood very well the powers of men in converting natural objects into artifacts, in utilizing and harnessing natural forces. As they understood man's powers, they were congenial to and compatible with nature because they were accommodations to and adjustments of nature. Human creativity was in harmony with or part of a unity with nature. The gods on the other hand, according to the popular opinion, worked miracles. Their creativity was incompatible with and opposed to nature. Their activities and efforts resulted in the amazing and marvelous. Men might grow corn, spin wool into cloth, sail ships, but all of these activities were accomplished according to the natural order. The gods, on the other hand, could turn corn into roses, make sheep talk, or capture the wind in a bag.

Machiavelli's new breed of men were to be men who combined the art of men and the gods, and thus would be demi-gods. Men, like the gods, could succeed in opposing nature, were not limited to achieving what the natural order had ordained for them. Men had unlimited potential because they could adapt to and resist a natural disorder. Fortune, a natural disorder, could, Machiavelli taught, be overcome by human virtue. An order, a political order, could be imposed upon a disorder by men who understood how to use the traditional virtues and vices well, by men who not only knew when to be cruel and when to be kind, who not only understood when to be violent and when to be peaceful, but who also possessed the will to act independently of nature. By these means an authority could be created, a rule established, a government constituted, which, like a shelter against the storm or a dam that holds back a turbulent river, would provide safety and security from the wild and violent natural forces that would otherwise have men at their mercy. Machiavelli thus claimed to be not only the founder of a new political philosophy but also the liberator of man because, by destroying the concept of nature as a limitation on being, he made men masters of the earth, creatures whose horizons were of their own making and thus capable of unlimited progress.

The modern philosophers not only revised the classical concept of nature but they also redefined the nature of man. Where the ancients had found man's distinctive characteristic to be a rationality that permitted men alone among the animals to know nature as a cosmos, a rationality that allowed men to distinguish the just from the unjust and the noble from the base, the moderns find man's distinctive characteristic to be the power of his will, a will that allows men to resist or overcome nature, a will that permits men to create an order and give meaning to a meaninglessness.

The moderns did not deny that man is rational, but they reduced the concept of rationality to calculation, and made reason the handservant of the passions. Reason no longer meant the power of true and right discernment: it was mere reckoning, the process of computing how to achieve what the will desired. As the ancients celebrated man's wisdom, so the moderns celebrated his freedom.

Thomas Hobbes, the first to follow Machiavelli's lead, defined man as the passion torn animal, restlessly seeking power after power.[15] The passions are dominant in man, said Hobbes, and there are two basic classes of passions, desire and aversion.[16] The human will is merely the last desire or aversion, that is, that desire or aversion upon which man acts.[17] The good is simply what we desire.[18] Thus, we do not desire something because we believe it is good, as the ancients argued. Rather, whatever we desire is good. There is, then, no objective good; nothing is good intrinsically; nothing is good in itself; goodness depends upon desire. Happiness is simply getting what you want continuously.[19] Since the good is whatever is desired, happiness has no objective content. The ends that men seek are too diverse to provide any direction. There is nothing intrinsically noble or just about happiness. It is not necessarily the life in accordance with virtue. If happiness has no definite substance, is not definable, then it cannot be the purpose of political associations to provide it. To provide happiness would be to give happiness an objective content, as the ancients did when they declared that happiness is the life in accordance with virtue. If the virtuous life is happiness, then governments can educate men to virtue. But if we do not know what will make each individual man happy, we cannot supply happiness, we can only provide the general conditions or prerequisites to it. Thus, political associations are not to secure happiness, but only the pursuit of happiness. Rationality or calculation discovers the prerequisites. To be happy one must first be, and thus, life is a necessary condition of happiness. Under the modern theory of the nature of man, the common good, the goal of political associations, is reduced from the good life to mere life.

Once the definition of the nature of man was revised, political philosophers would take an entirely new perspective on the value of nature and convention. In declaring rationality to be the peculiar excellence of man, the ancients had found human life to be purposive, and its purpose was established and limited by something outside of and higher than men—the ordered whole, the cosmos of which man was a part and that he could seek to understand. A man could begin to discover the purpose of human life; he could discover what he was for, what gave life meaning. The moderns' new definition of the nature of man, centering on the power or freedom of the human will, at once destroys the limitations on man and makes life purposeless. In so doing it provides men with the task of creating a meaning for life, of founding an order. Life is not an expedition, a journey with a definite purpose; it is an adventure, a spontaneous activity. The emphasis shifted from understanding human life to experiencing and managing it.

Chapter 6

THE MODERNS

Political Things are Conventional

Why has government been instituted at all? Because the passions of men will not conform to the dictates of reason and justice, without constraint.

Alexander Hamilton

Machiavelli changed the meaning of the term nature, and he was so successful in altering men's perspectives on this ultimate reality that his intellectual descendant, Thomas Hobbes, was able to base his entire political philosophy on a conquest of nature. While Machiavelli speaks of fortune as originally controlling half of the affairs of men and thus constituting a naturally occurring condition on or antecedent to the will of men, Hobbes speaks of a state of nature as the original mode of human existence.[1] Fully accepting Machiavelli's implicit argument that nature is not a positive standard, that there is nothing praiseworthy or excellent in the way things are or in the way things are originally, Hobbes posits nature as the ultimate negative standard. Nature is not the *summum bonum* (the highest good) as the ancients had maintained; nature is the *summum malum* (the greatest evil).[2] Nature is not an end, it is a beginning, and progress can be measured in terms of our distance from this original negative pole.

The state of nature, according to Hobbes, is a state of the war of the all against the all[3], every man at war with every other man simultaneously. As a negative pole, it is completely successful; a more terrible condition is beyond thought. In the state of nature men are abjectly miserable, for life is "solitary, poor, nasty, brutish, and short."[4] Such a standard absolutely assures progress for anything at all is better. Even tyranny, which Aristotle found to be the greatest political evil, begins to look like a pleasing alternative. The state of nature is civil war, which, as Thucydides said, produces "every form of depravity", taken to its logical extreme.[5]

The state of nature is informed by one fundamental "law" —preserve yourself.[6] It is not a law properly so-called but rather a natural instinct. It is as much the way or character of man as two legs or two eyes. The state of nature is a state of the war of the all against the all because it is a state of perfect rights, a state of perfect anarchy, a state of perfect equality, and a state of perfect freedom.

It is a state of perfect rights because all men have a right to everything they need to secure their own preservation.[7] This means that men have no duties to each other. All duties circumscribe and limit rights. If I have a perfect right to speak freely, I have no duty to allow you to speak. If you have a perfect right to life, you have a perfect right to take anything that is a means to that end whether it be food, shelter, or even my life.

The state of nature is a state of perfect anarchy because all men are kings of the earth. There is no common judge among them, no authority of any kind over any one of them.[8] Each man decides what means are necessary to preserve himself, and so every man rules himself and is ruled by no man. All men are at once kings of the earth, but they are kings without subjects. All rule, no one obeys. Since no one is ruled, the state of nature is a state of anarchy—the absence of government of any kind.

It is a state of perfect equality because all men are identical in the only thing that matters, susceptibility to murder.[9] Every man can kill every other man. Even the weakest man can kill the strongest if he comes upon him while he is asleep. None of the attributes by which men make distinctions among themselves, not wisdom, nor virtue, nor speed, nor strength, nor beauty, provide invulnerability to violent attack. Since they do not, these attributes are irrelevant. Men may be unequal in the highest things, as was patently the observation of the ancients, but Hobbes' response is, "So what!" The observable differences of body and mind have no significance when judged by the fundamental standard and sole common purpose of men—mere life, mere preservation.

The state of nature is a state of perfect freedom because there are no restrictions that bind any man's will.[10] No man is his brother's keeper, no man has any responsibilities toward another nor bears another's burdens. No man has any claim on another or any authority over another. In the state of nature a man *may* do whatever he *can* do. The phrase "I should" has no meaning in the state of nature other than "I can, I will" or "it pleases me."

All this results in the state of the war of the all against the all. The universality of rights means the complete clash of rights. The sovereignty of all makes each man the final judge in his own cause, and men are notoriously bad judges in their own causes. The fundamental equality of mortality is an invitation to violence, and natural freedom is a license to murder. The only good thing about the state of nature is that men can leave it, and they do so by building on that pure and incorruptible passion, the fear of violent death.

Men construct a government, create a common judge by giving up some of their natural rights, some of their natural equality, some of their natural freedom.[11] They make a contract in which by giving up some of their rights they take on duties, by giving up their equal sovereignty they become subjects and citizens, by giving up some of their freedom they accept restraints and laws. They do this in exchange for peace, for an end of the war of the all against the all.[12] Political things are, then, not natural. Government is artificial, conventional, a construct, a manmade thing, built and formed by men as an act of will to overcome the defects of nature. Political things are the first and perhaps the greatest evidence of man's conquest of nature.

Hobbes' argument for the artificiality of political things rests primarily on his logical account of how political things come to be by the conscious deliberate action of men. Natural things do not come to be, according to the modern perception; they are original, the first stage of existence, and thus the source of all subsequent stages of existence. That subsequent stages of existence do follow the original stage is explained by the second major premise of Hobbes' account: nature is not only the first stage of existence rather than the last stage of existence, it is the most imperfect stage of existence rather than the most perfect. Since it is the most imperfect stage and since its imperfections frustrate the natural human passion for self-preservation, men will not long endure its defects and will act deliberately and independently to overcome them.

JOHN LOCKE

John Locke, the foremost proponent of limited or constitutional government, not only accepted Hobbes' two major premises but made them respectable, ironically while appearing to reject them. Locke accepts without argument the moderns' premise that nature is the first or original condition of men. Like Hobbes, he bases his political theory on a state of nature, arguing that, "to understand political power right and derive it from its *original,* we must consider what state all men are naturally in. . . ."[13] This fundamental revision of the ancients' definition of nature was so firmly established by the late seventeenth century that for all practical purposes it ceased to be a point of dispute. However, the second major Hobbesian premise, that the state of nature was the worst condition of men, continued to be debated in part because it was diametrically opposed to the received theological beliefs of the Judeo-

Christian tradition, which taught of perfect beginnings in God's perfect world, the Garden of Eden.

The judicious Locke by subtle circumlocution delivers the second premise from the disgrace of unorthodoxy. He begins by accentuating the apparent positive about the state of nature—that it is a state of perfect freedom and equality.[14] He imbues the state of nature with a legalistic aura by stating the law of nature in its most benign form (the law which "wills the peace and preservation of all mankind") and proceeds to analyze it as if it were a prescriptive rather than a descriptive rule.[15] In particular, by speaking of sanctions, reparations, retributions for transgressions, punishment, and, above all, the execution and enforcement of the law of nature, he converts a law that describes what men in fact do and cannot be expected not to do into a law that appears to prescribe what men ought to do as if it were a moral duty.[16]

The state of nature appears in this way to be a rather noble place governed by a noble rule: preserve yourself and others when your own preservation is not threatened.[17] That it is actually not noble, according to Locke, is only vaguely hinted at. The law of nature, however noble it may sound in Locke's first account of it, has one grave defect: it is not fully known or, rather, it is both known and unknown, or it is known only to a "studier."[18] This is a grave problem because men can in no way *obey* unknown laws, and they cannot be expected to obey unknown laws. If the law of nature is, contrary to Locke's presentation of it, descriptive, written on the hearts of men, if it is the way or nature of men to preserve themselves, then the law of nature is "known" to all men. If, however, it is merely a descriptive law, like the laws of gravity or planetary motion, then it is ridiculous to speak of sanctions and punishments for deviating from the law.

When descriptive laws are broken we do not punish the deviators; we change or modify the law. If one of the planets does not move, as the law of planetary motion tells us it will move, we do not raise our voices in shouts of indignation and calls for punishment, we do not see defect in the motion but rather defect in the law. On the other hand, if the law of nature is a law men can be expected to obey and justly punished for disobeying, as Locke presents it, a prescriptive law, then it must be promulgated, officially announced, publicized. Knowledge of the law of nature cannot be limited to studiers or experts if it is to rule the behavior of men.

The solution to the problem posed by Locke's manner of presenting the law of nature is implied in his distinction between two different manifestations of the law: the executive power and the judicial power. All men are, according to Locke, the executives or executors of the law of nature.[19] All men are executors of the law of nature in the descriptive sense—preserving themselves is what men in fact do and cannot be expected not to do. In exercising the executive power, men "know" the law of nature or the law of nature is accurate in describing what men in fact do.

On the other hand, all men exercise the judicial power, the power of judging what is lawful and what is not, of judging what particular specific actions uphold and fulfill the law, and what particular specific actions are destructive of or in "violation" of the law.[20] Since each man possesses the judicial power, every man is a judge in his own case. Herein lies the rub. As judges in their own cases, men are neither disinterested nor dispassionate. In short, they are notoriously bad judges. They are frequently mistaken as to what particular specific actions will actually preserve themselves.

The possibility of error is magnified because a man must judge not only whether another is an actual aggressor but also whether another is a potential aggressor.[21] If a man comes toward you with a rock or a club, makes a direct overt attack, you will probably not be mistaken in concluding that he threatens your being. But, absent direct overt attack, how do you judge without error when a man hates you, when he has such "an enmity to [your] being" that he may attack indirectly or covertly, catching you unaware or asleep? Correct judgment here is important because in the state of nature all men possess the executive power, the power of acting to enforce their judgments. The judicial power informs and directs the executive power. A man is either a threat to you or he is not, but do you have reliable knowledge one way or the other? Should you take preventative action, make the first move, or should you wait and see? If you wait and see, you may be increasing the risk to your life. If you take preventative action, you may be needlessly increasing the general level of violence and distrust. You must make a judgment, and, according to Locke, in such a case, a man is more likely to decide his own preservation takes precedence. He will accept the risk of needlessly increasing the general level of violence, the risk that he has misjudged another man, in order to avoid the risk to his own life. The "evils which necessarily follow from men's being judges in their own cases" convert the state of nature from an apparently noble condition into a state "not to be endured."[22] As judges in their own cases, all men direct their behavior, all men determine what they "ought" to do, but they do not judge well. Since they do not judge well, they do not actually know the law of nature in the prescriptive sense of conforming their behavior to the rule.

The law of nature is thus defective because it is not fully known to all. The state of nature is actually not a noble condition but rather an unendurable condition governed by a defective law. The defect in the law of nature is the universality of the judicial power. Too many judges spoil the state of nature. If that is the defect, then the remedy is clear: a common judge —a government. If the problem is that each by nature is the final judge in his own cause, that there is no natural authority, then the solution is to give up the judicial power, to create an authority. This authority, not occurring in nature, must be a construct, a manmade thing. Therefore, political things are not natural. By suggesting at first that the state of nature is governed by a noble law, and then gradually revealing the defectiveness of that law, Locke mitigates the harsh appearance of

Hobbes' teaching about the state of nature while retaining its substance.

In a like fashion, he proves the state of nature is identical to a state of war while professing to demonstrate the "plain difference" between the two.[23] He does this by giving new and, he says, proper definitions of the state of nature and the state of war. The state of nature properly so-called is defined by the absence of a common judge.[24] By nature, all men have the right to judge what is necessary for their preservation, to decide what fulfills the law of nature. The presence of a common judge would signify an unnatural state or the state of civil society. By convention or contract, men commission public officers to decide conflicts and controversies and give their enforcement proxies to the police and the courts. The state of war properly so-called is defined by the use of force without right, both where there is and is not a common judge.[25] To use force without right is either an act of unwarranted aggression against another (as when, in the state of nature, a man uses force although he and his are not actually threatened by another) or a failure to keep a freely given promise (as when, in the state of civil society, a man uses force to punish another who has injured him or his instead of leaving the punishment to the courts). In the first case, the use of force is contrary to the natural law, which allows a man to use force to protect his life and property, but only when these are in jeopardy, since it ordains that men shall preserve others as well as themselves. In the second case, the use of force is contrary to the social contract through which men gave up the right to use force. The state of peace is, therefore, the state where force is not used without right. In this state, force would only be used for self-defense or by the authorities created by the contract—the courts and the police. To summarize:

1. The state of nature = the absence of a common judge.
2. The state of civil society = the presence of the common judge.

3. The state of war = the use of force without right both where there is and is not a common judge.
4. The state of peace = no use of force without right.

While this purports to teach us "the plain difference" between the state of nature and the state of war, it in fact does the opposite.

By declaring that the state of war can exist both where there is and is not a common judge, Locke seems to suggest that the state of war is not unique to or identical with the state of nature. We may ask, how can the state of war exist in civil society where there is a common judge with the authority to prevent the use of force without right? The answer is that in civil society the authority of the common judge is not always and everywhere effective and efficient.[26] It is not always operative. Many a man has yelled, "Help! Police!," and there is no police officer, no common judge nearby to prevent the use of force without right. In such a situation, a man reverts to the state of nature; the absence of a common judge makes him the judge in his own case. Force without right occurs only when the common judge is absent or ineffectual. Therefore, force without right, the state of war, can occur only in the state of nature precisely defined as the absence of a common judge. Locke agrees completely with Hobbes on the point that the state of nature is a state of war. Nature is a condition of "enmity, malice, violence and mutual destruction."[27] It is clearly more than an inconvenient and ineffective condition; it is a miserable and unendurable condition.

Locke, apparently not satisfied with the miseries of violence and destruction, discovers more—the miseries of abject poverty. Characteristically, he makes a propitious beginning. God, he says, gave the earth to men in common.[28] We are vast land holders all, and as a result, apparently well off if not actually rich. Locke's language in this context is certainly reassuring. He speaks of support and comfort, fruits, nourishment, and production by the spontaneous hand of nature.[29] It sounds very good, as though we have been blessed indeed. All we have to do is to appropriate, to take for our own use from an apparent plenty spontaneously produced. There is a catch, however, —appropriation is nothing more than an euphemism for the labor of gathering and harvesting, a labor so necessary that without it the commonly owned earth is useless. Still the fact that there is a natural plenty to harvest would mean that the labor of collecting was not particularly burdensome or oppressive, and that the contribution of men was not especially significant.

The natural plenty, it turns out, is a mirage. It begins to disappear as we look at it more closely. If men can labor in the form of collecting the spontaneously-produced fruits of the earth, men can labor in the form of cultivating, tilling, and planting. As every farmer's son knows, more corn is produced on cultivated land than by the spontaneous acts of nature. In fact, cultivated land yields ten times more, nay says Locke, a hundred times more, a thousand times more.[30] Without labor the earth is worthless. There is no natural plenty. Plenty is manmade, a product of human labor. God was a stingy gift-giver.

Labor is the source of all value, and labor is, according to Locke, the source of private property.[31] By appropriating, and by the labor he invests, a man removes something from the common and makes it his own.[32] How much may a man remove from the common? As much as he can use before it spoils and thereby wastes not only his neighbor's share but his own labor.[33] The potential yield of labor is clearly so great that men using reason to calculate their advantage decided by "tacit agreement" to invent money.[34] The invention of money (gold does not rot) overcomes the spoilage limit and releases the phenomenal productivity of human labor.

Since some men are stronger, more energetic, or more industrious than others, the decision to release labor from the spoilage limit is clearly an agreement to inequality of property. Differences in human ability or character were insignificant prior to the invention of money because, given the spoilage limit and the other "inconveniences" of the state of nature, they had little or no consequences. One man might be able to eat twice or thrice as much as another and thus gather or plant and use three times as much as another before his harvest decayed, but no man could consume a hundred, nay a thousand times more than another.

Despite our egalitarian prejudices, and despite the natural equality of man's original condition, Locke contends that the agreement to inequality in property is highly rational. Labor is the source of all value, for "of the products of the earth useful to the life of man . . . ninety-nine hundreds are wholly to be put on the account of labor."[35] A man has a right to the product of his labor, and indeed were the product denied him, he would have, according to Locke, no incentive to labor. Though all do not share the plenty equally, all are better off because of the agreement to "a disproportional and unequal possession of the earth."[36] How are men better off? They are better off materially because there is simply more of everything; they are better off to the extent that "bread is worth more than acorns, wine than water, and cloth or silk than leaves, skins, or moss."[37] The invention of money is in a sense the invention of inequality, but to give up one's equal right to the earth is merely to give up one's right to destitution. The equality of the state of nature is worthless. Men are in grave need, malnourished and miserable in their natural condition. They live just at the starvation line, if they manage to live at all. Living not in simple poverty but in abject penury on nuts and berries and water, man in the state of nature is truly wretched.

Exercising great care not to offend the conventional wisdom and prevailing religious pieties, Locke, like Hobbes, concludes that nature is not only the original condition of men, but the worst condition. It is a negative pole, a negative standard. All utility, all worth and all value are produced by labor, and thus, what man has made, the artificial, the conventional, is an improvement upon and an achievement against nature.

Rousseau

The two major premises of modernity on the state of nature having been established and rendered respectable, were now ripe for schism. The division occurred at the hands of Jean-Jacques Rousseau, one of the most influential of all modern philosophers. The focal point of the division in modern thought is the second premise that nature is a negative pole. Like Locke before him, Rousseau does not question the first premise that nature is the original condition of man. In fact, the schism occurred because Rousseau fully agreed with Hobbes and Locke that the state of nature is the original condition of men. What he did question is whether they had actually discovered the state of nature.[38] He argues they did not, and because they did not, they mistakenly set up nature as a negative pole.

Hobbes had begun his famous description of the state of nature by saying that the life of man is solitary—that is, men lived in the presence of others but not in fellowship, harmony, sympathy, or association with others. Rousseau not only concurs but maintains that the life of man is radically solitary.[39] In the state of nature, men live entirely alone, so completely segregated from one another as to make the propagation of the species somewhat unexpected. Men pass their lives not merely in a private aloofness but, except for brief sexual encounters that do continue the species, totally without social intercourse. They live unaccompanied, unattended, and unacquainted with any of their kind. They do not live together in families, or bands, or tribes; they live in complete isolation from each other. Hobbes and Locke, says Rousseau, were wrong about the state of nature because the life they describe is not solitary. It is a fiercely and violently competitive struggle for existence, and competition requires the presence of and interaction with others.

If life in the state of nature is truly solitary, if it is radically asocial, then men don't interact at all; they do not commit acts of violence and theft upon each other; they do not live in fear of each other. The radical separation of men means there is little if any occasion for violence. Men who live in solitude do not present any threat to each other. And so, Hobbes was wrong; life in the state of nature is not violent. Furthermore, in order to live in such total seclusion from each other, originally there must be few men. If there are few men, then the spontaneous production of nature can supply their simple needs for food and shelter.[40] Poverty does not exist because, with so few demands upon it, the natural supply is adequate to sustain life. Any thought of supply beyond mere subsistence is nonexistent because men do not think.[41] They do not think because they do not possess language.[42] Language and reason presuppose each other. You can't have one without the other. Language presupposes society, some form of association that allows meanings to be consistently applied to certain sounds or symbols. Language is a public thing; it is not and cannot be absolutely private. Since life in the state of nature is not merely private but solitary, men do not possess language and thus cannot reason. Since nature spontaneously produces enough to sustain mere life when there are few men, and since men cannot think of excess or wealth or of a possible future shortage, Locke is wrong; the state of nature is not a state of abject poverty.

Although men cannot think, they are conscious, that is they are aware of their existence. They know that they are, and they find pleasure in being.[43] They are moved by only two passions, both of which are directly connected to the conscious perception of the sweetness of being—the desire for self-preservation and a natural pity or compassion at the suffering of others.[44] There is no conflict between these two basic natural passions. The desire for self-preservation does not overcome or destroy natural pity because men are solitary, self-sufficient, and equal. The different talents of men have no meaning because they have no manifestations, no products, no results. Strength and speed in the state of nature have no meaning since they have no effects. Solitary men do not compete and have no occasion to measure and compare talents. The state of nature is neither a state of war nor a state of abject poverty. It is not and cannot be a negative pole.

On the contrary, the state of nature is a positive pole, according to Rousseau. This is a more difficult concept to grasp because, while life in the state of nature is pleasant, according to Rousseau's account, it is a subhuman or prehuman life. Almost all the particularly human things, the things we have treasured about mankind, the things that the poets and statesmen have praised in men—love, friendship, honor, courage, loyalty, rationality, morality—all these things are missing in the state of nature. On what basis then can Rousseau offer the state of nature as a positive pole?

Rousseau's answer is on the basis of the freedom of the state of nature. Man is perfectly free in the state of nature, by which Rousseau means he is totally independent, undetermined, and conscious of his freedom.[45] He is free because he can choose what he will be and what he will do without any restraint from nature or man. Animals are largely ruled by instinct; thus they are largely determined; but man is a plastic creature and therefore perfectible. He can adapt and add things to himself; he can change his way of being as animals cannot.

Although the terms Rousseau uses, "freedom" and "perfectibility," connote approval and thereby support Rousseau's contention that nature is a positive pole, man's freedom or his perfectibility are merely raw potential, capacity or power simply without regard for its use or its purpose or the direction of its development. Vice is as much the possible product of man's perfectibility as virtue. Perfectibility is the potential to do evil as well as good. Natural man is, according to Rousseau, an indefinite and unlimited creature, a creature who can become anything. It is this undirected potential, this capacity without a terminus, that is unique to man and that makes nature a positive pole. Nature has made man the only creature capable of developing his own nature. Man's freedom then is not only independence but creativity.

If natural man is radically free and if, as observation tells us, men are not radically free in civil society, civil society is neither natural nor simply desirable. Civil society is a product of human activity, it is a human contrivance, and men have not done well by themselves. According to Rousseau, men left the state of nature and in the process exchanged a contented mode of existence for a less happy one.[46] Misfortune, chance, or accident interrupted man's solitude, forcing men into closer and closer contact with their fellows.[47] Natural catastrophies, climatological changes, droughts, or perhaps an ice age reduced the area of inhabitable land, decreased the spontaneously-produced supply of food. When nature no longer satisfied their wants, men began to take an active part in the satisfaction of their needs.[48] Proximity permitted recognition of common needs, and produced cooperation, which in turn gave birth to obligation. Men thus invented associations and society. Speech and reason developed as did vanity, violence, and inequality.

Violence arises because proximity and the development of speech and reason made conflicts of interest and quarrels possible. Scarcity, failure to fulfill obligations, trespass, insult—all these and more lead to bloodshed. Vanity arises because proximity also permitted comparisons and comparisons led to competition, which spotlighted the hitherto almost invisible differences in the faculties of men.[49] The strong, the swift, the talented, the clever, and the beautiful came to be admired and envied. Men proceeded to develop and enhance these attributes in order to earn greater admiration. Applause, approval, and even love became psychological necessities. The sweetness of simple being no longer satisfied. To be, without friends, without family, without respect, without recognition, is to be miserable, and men began to think that without these things it might be better not to be. Inequality arises in the first instance because of comparisons and competition for approval, but in the second and most important instance because of the invention of private property.[50] Here Rousseau fully agrees with Locke on the origin (though not the value) of private property. The invention of agriculture, the introduction of human labor, creates inequality because labor is the source of private property and because unequal human talents, when expressed in the form of labor, can be converted into something tangible—into wheat and wine, into yachts and race cars, in a word, into money.[51] O. J. Simpson's speed, Robert Redford's profile and Henry Ford's cleverness can procure wealth as well as simple admiration. In fact, says Rousseau, the first man, who fenced off and through his labor claimed as his own a section of the commonly-owned earth, was the "true founder of civil society."[52] If only, laments Rousseau, someone had knocked down that first fence, "what crimes, wars, murders, what miseries and horrors would the human race have been spared."[53]

Men added to their natures, appending properties and features to themselves that both ennobled and debased their characters. If men by socializing themselves made loyalty possible, so did they make betrayal possible. If the invention of society made the enlightment possible, permitted the development of reason and perhaps even the achievement of wisdom, it also destroyed man's independence, enslaving men through their acquired needs to the assistance and good opinion of others. Men were no longer free because they were no longer self-sufficient. They had developed new needs that could only be satisfied by other men, and so they had to live for others.[54]

When men left the state of nature, when they gave direction and substance to their raw potential, they created history, a series of events and points of development in time. Men made things happen, whereas in the state of nature nothing had happened. Life had had a pleasant dreamlike quality; men were idle, human will was dormant, there was no story of man because nothing had come to pass.

Rousseau is a modern philosopher because he agrees with the moderns that nature is the original condition of men and that political things are created by men and thus are unnatural. But, he disagrees with the moderns' conclusion that nature is a negative pole. To Rousseau the state of nature is a positive pole because in the state of nature: 1) Men's needs are satisfied;

their needs are few and nature supplies them spontaneously. 2) Men do no harm and are content in enjoying the simple consciousness of the sweetness of their existence. 3) Men are independent and perfectible—they are free.

Civil society, what man hath wrought, is an undesirable condition because it makes men bad by making them dependent upon each other. The development of reason permits men to calculate their own advantage in terms of the disadvantage of others. Calculation of self-interest produces the thought that when he is injured, I am stronger. Thus, man's natural compassion or natural regret at the misfortune of others is overcome. Civil society is undesirable because it legitimates inequalities. Sociality allows different talents to emerge and to have effects. These talents become useful in obtaining the good opinion and the assistance of others. Civil society is undesirable because it has enslaved men, and alienated them from themselves. Men live for the good opinion of others. They need others not only in terms of sharing the burdens of maintaining life, but also to feed their vanity, to give them status and applause.

If, however, civil society is a contrivance, created by men, it can be controlled or reshaped by men. If men have lost their natural freedom in the process of developing their humanity, they can reestablish freedom by their own art. They can create an artificial or conventional freedom informed by their understanding of the state of nature as a positive pole.

Chapter 7

THE MODERNS
The Science of Government

Concern for man himself and his fate must always form the chief
interest of all technical endeavors, concern for the great unsolved
problems of the organization of labor and the distribution of
goods—in order that the creations of our mind shall be a blessing
and not a curse to mankind.

Albert Einstein

Modern political philosophers also raised the question,
Are political things natural? After a thorough and systematic
examination of the issue, they answered, No, political things are
not natural; they are conventional. There is no natural title to
rule; there are no natural rulers. Thus, the best regime simply
becomes, for the moderns, a fiction, an imaginary republic. The
basic principles of government cannot be discovered but rather
must be invented or constructed.

Even though the modern political philosophers of the
mainstream denied natural authority, they did not deny the
concept of nature. Man, after all, did not create himself or the
world—some things are given even if they are only the raw
materials for human creativity. Man may not have a political
nature, but he does have a nature. Political things may be
manufactured, but they are manufactured out of something.
Man may be a creator, but his creativity is of a different order
than that of the gods, who produce something out of nothing.

Despite their disagreements with the ancient political philosophers about the naturalness of political things, and despite their disagreements among themselves about the positive/negative characteristics of the state of nature, the modern political philosophers of the mainstream agree with the ancients that the nature of man is the proper standard for evaluating political things. The philosophers of the mainstream, ancient and modern, utilize the nature of man as the appropriate yardstick of political life.

THE MAJORITY OPINION

The primal moment, the state of nature, is the primitive and crude beginning. The moderns, however, disagreed about the value of this original condition, with the majority finding it to be a negative pole, the worst possible condition. Politics has to do with ruling and being ruled. A rule binds behavior, constrains conduct and designates duties. Since political things are not natural, there are no duties in the state of nature, or *every* man has a right to *all* things.[1] Natural right is, then, the basic characteristic of the state of nature, the elemental fact about the nature of man. Since the universality of natural rights means the total conflict of rights, natural right is the problem to be solved by man's creativity.

The ancient political philosophers did not have to face this problem because they had no theory of a state of nature or of natural rights. They would have called the state of nature an imaginary condition, or a subhuman condition. Man, said Aristotle, is the political animal. All human rights flow from human duties. Rights and duties are reciprocal. There are no human rights that predate civil society.

The majority opinion of the moderns is that the state of nature is the *summum malum,* the war of the all against the all. Reason or calculation of self-interest tells us that we must leave it as soon as possible, which is to say that we must relinquish some natural rights. The problem of giving up natural rights is a complex one and can be broken down into several questions: How can natural rights be given up? What natural rights can be given up? To whom or what shall they be given? What is the consequence of giving up natural rights?

How Can Natural Rights Be Relinquished?

According to Thomas Hobbes, natural rights can be relinquished by a mutual agreement among men called the *social contract.*[2] This agreement, which is an act of will on the part of each individual, creates reciprocal obligations. The social contract is a primary law and an act of self-legislation.[3] Since each man has a natural right to all things, no one can impose a duty or enforce a rule upon any individual except the individual himself. Thus all genuine law is and must be self-legislation. To give up a natural right is to consent to a duty. The act must be voluntary and so the *only* title to rule, according to modern political thought, is consent—consent and nothing else. All of the natural-rights philosophers, including Hobbes, Locke, and Rousseau, agree that the social contract is based upon the consent of individuals.[4]

What Natural Rights Can Be Given Up?

Almost all natural rights can be relinquished or transferred. There must, however, be some non-transferable rights since natural rights are the basic element in man's nature.[5] If all rights could be alienated, then man would not have a nature. Because man has a natural right to all things, the simplest way of proceeding is to discover which rights are inalienable. The primary right is the right to life, which is the *sine qua non* of all other rights. Without the right to life, all other rights are nugatory. If any right is inalienable it must be this. So, all modern natural-right theory is based on the premise that life is an inalienable right of man.

Hobbes

Thomas Hobbes, the father of modern liberalism, bases his entire theory of government upon this simple premise: self-preservation is the inalienable right of man. According to Hobbes, when men make the social contract they give up all their rights except this one and, of course, anything that can be narrowly construed from it.[6] They thereby create an almost perfect obligation for themselves. In the state of nature, men possessed perfect rights; under the social contract, they have agreed to an almost perfect duty. The exceptions to this duty are simple and obvious.[7] Every man has the right of resistance; that is, he is not bound to obey an executioner, to submit dutifully to his own demise. He is not bound to obey any order that would lead to his certain death. Further, he is not obligated to do anything that would make his own life abhorrent to him, such as to kill his mother, to eat human flesh, or to maim himself.

Short of cooperating in his own death or engaging in an act that would fill him with loathing for his own life, a man gives up all his other natural rights when he makes the social contract. Specifically, according to Hobbes (with the above exception), he gives up the judicial power, the power of judging good and evil, and he gives up the executive power, the power of enforcing his judgment, or more simply, he gives up the right to use force.[8] There is no legislative power in nature since there is no natural authority, or there is no such thing as a law made by men in the state of nature. The act of legislating is coeval with the moment of leaving the state of nature.

The significance of alienating the judicial power or of transferring the right to judge is that once the social contract is made there is no right of revolution.[9] No one can retain his private idea of justice. No one has a right to pronounce judgment upon a political regime and overthrow it by force. Every man has given up the right of personal judgment. The right of resistance remains, but this is an *individual* right not a collective one, and it is severely circumscribed because it is limited to the extreme case, to the case where there is a "clear and present danger" of death.

Locke

John Locke, who is more commonly thought of as the founder of modern liberalism, agrees with Hobbes that life is the inalienable right. He differs from Hobbes in that he broadly construes this right, or he discovers two other inalienable rights.[10] If there is anything one has a right to, or to put it in Lockean terms, if there is anything that belongs to an individual, it is his life. A man has an inalienable *property* right in his being or in his person. By extension, he also has a property right in his liberty, that is, the right to control his own person for his own benefit. Finally, he has a property right in that with which he mixes his person, or in the products of his own labor. Thus the Lockean formula for inalienable natural rights is: life, liberty and estate, the latter euphemistically termed "the pursuit of happiness" by Thomas Jefferson.

Since Locke broadly construes the inalienable right of life to include liberty, and since liberty means self-determination or the right to make decisions regarding the use of one's own person, man could not and did not wholly give up the judicial power of nature when he made the social contract.[11] He did, however, wholly give up the executive power, but not in the first instance to the government.[12] This means that there is a right of revolution.[13] The right of revolution is, like all natural rights, a prepolitical right. The difference between Hobbes and Locke on this issue of the right of revolution derives from Locke's separation of society and government. According to Locke, the social contract creates civil society, which in turn forms a government. When a man gives up the executive power of nature, he irrevocably gives up his right to enforce his own private will, and he transfers this right of enforcement to the civil society.[14] The civil society then transfers (as an act of delegation and not of alienation) the executive power to the government.[15]

The result is that police, the magistrates, and ultimately the government, have everyman's proxy. While the government stands, it and it alone has the right to use force. The police have your proxy, and you can never go down to the police station and get it back. Nonetheless, the police do not necessarily have your proxy forever. You cannot get it back but civil society can.[16] By separating society and government and by making society superior to government, Locke's social contract theory allows for revolution, the overthrow of the government or more aptly the taking back of the executive power. Further, it allows for revolution without destroying the social contract, without returning to individual men the natural right of the executive power. It is society that takes back the power to use force, and thus the right of revolution is a *collective* or community right, the right of the majority and not an individual right.[17] The individual right to use force is a natural right that men alienated, gave up forever when they made the social contract. When society takes back the power to use force, it does so only to invest it in another government.

To Whom or What Shall Natural Rights Be Given?

Hobbes

According to Hobbes, all relinquished natural rights are given to the sovereign, or the sovereign is the name given to that man or group of men to whom the natural rights are trans-ferred.[18] The sovereign, then, has more rights than anyone else. As Hobbes understood it, the social contract is made in order to create a sovereign, a superior, supreme power. The defect of nature is the lack of a natural authority. Each man gave up certain natural rights and in so doing promised that he would not exercise those rights again or, to put it in other terms, promised that he would assume certain duties.[19] Each man gave his promise on the condition that every other man gave a similar promise.[20] Promises are assurances of future behavior, and so the social contract is a trust. In order for the social contract to have any force, there must be a belief in the faithful performance of promises, or there must be a guarantee of performance.[21] This is the role of the sovereign—he is the guarantee of future performance. The social contract is made out of self-interest. If a man perceives a change in his self-interest, he might renege, break his promise. To prevent this, the sovereign is created, and he is there to see to it that a man has more to lose by breaking his contract than by keeping it.

The sovereign, according to Hobbes, can do this because he is not a party to the contract, because he has the monopoly of rights.[22] The sovereign is not a party to the social contract because he does not exist until the contract is made. The contract is not an agreement between the subjects and the sovereign; rather, it is an agreement among equals to create a sovereign, to create an inequality. As a result, the sovereign has no duties because he has retained *all* his natural rights.

This very abstract way of looking at the relationship of the sovereign to his subjects can perhaps be better understood by analogy. Assume that ten men have ten marbles each, and that each man decides to give away nine marbles on the condition that all of them do likewise. There is a pool of ninety marbles. They then draw lots or by some other device assign the pool of ninety marbles to one of the ten. This means that nine men have one marble each, and the tenth man has 91 marbles. He gets back the nine he put into the pool plus 81 more. This in simplistic form is Hobbes' conception of the sovereign's position under the social contract. The sovereign retains *all of his own* natural rights and is granted all of those natural rights relinquished by others. He thus has a monopoly of rights, or is the superior of every man. The social contract is made to create a superior since the defect of nature is simple equality or the lack of a natural authority.

Although each man retains one right, the right of self-preservation, which in civil society includes the right of resistance, the retention of this right does not defeat the purpose of the contract. The contract is made to set up a common judge, the sovereign, who, possessing a monopoly of rights including the right to use force, maintains peace, the condition absolutely necessary for individual self-preservation.[23] The social contract, thus, reduces the conflict of rights that occurs in nature to a bare minimum. The only conflict of rights that can occur is the conflict between the sovereign, who has the right to order an execution, and the individual to be executed, who has a right to resist. Since the right of resistance is an individual and not a collective right (a man may rightfully resist the sovereign only when his own life is in danger and not when someone else's life is in danger) the breach of the peace that occurs because of this conflict of rights is slight.

The sovereign has absolute rights; his will is law.[24] Even the right of resistance does not seriously handicap the exercise of his rights. Clearly this sovereign is a convincing guarantee of the contract. The parties to the contract will have more to lose by breaking their promises than by keeping them. But, what is there to prevent an arbitrary and dictatorial rule? According to Hobbes, there is the self-interest of the sovereign— his self-interest in remaining the sovereign.[25] If he debilitates his subjects, he can be defeated in war. If he abuses his subjects, they will rebel. They do not have the right to rebel, but they will, nonetheless. If he abuses too many individual men or if too many individuals exercise their right of resistance at a given time, the power of the sovereign may not be sufficient to control them. Law is the will of the sovereign, and the sovereign and thus the law lasts as long as the power of the sovereign lasts. This principle is easily seen in a schoolyard where the smaller boys attach themselves to and serve as "go-fers" for the biggest and toughest boy. They live securely in the shadow of his protection. But, if a big and tough new boy takes on their protector and defeats him, the newcomer becomes the ruler of the schoolyard, and the smaller boys shift their attachment to him—his will becomes their law. Self-preservation is a primary principle and overrides loyalty and gratitude for past benefits. Power is the basis of all ruling.[26]

Locke

Locke follows Hobbes part way down this road, but only part way. The natural rights which are relinquished are given to a sovereign body called civil society.[27]

The social contract is a trust, and civil society is the guarantee of future performance. Civil society by majority vote creates a government that has the delegated authority to use force in order to compel individuals to fulfill their obligations.[28] Government is merely the executor of the will of civil society. At any time, civil society can take back the authority it has delegated and appoint a new government. Government is thus limited, not absolute, or Locke's theory is one of constitutional government.[29]

The social contract is made to minimize the conflict of rights that makes the state of nature the war of the all against the all. The Hobbesian remedy of absolute government is, according to Locke, worse than the disease. In the state of nature, the equality of right means that each man is in a conflict of right with every other man individually, but under absolute government each man can be in a conflict of right with the whole organized body of men, as when the absolute sovereign arbitrarily orders an execution. In such a case, a man actually has a better chance of exercising his right to life in the state of nature, where men are unorganized and there is no obligation to assist anyone else, than he has under an absolute sovereign who can command everyone of his subjects to assist his executioner. In nature you play one on one; under absolute government you play one against a whole team. A man cannot rationally agree to worsen his condition, and therefore, a man cannot consent to absolute government.[30]

Except for absolute government, any other form of government is possible.[31] Indeed, the form doesn't matter. Civil society by a majority vote creates a government. It can create a monarchy, an oligarchy, a democracy or a mixed regime. Any form that protects property (life, liberty, and estate) and that is approved by a majority is legitimate. The problem of arbitrary or dictatorial government is resolved by separating society and government.[32] If the government is abusive, society always has the right of revolution, which is actually the act of taking back a delegated power. The true rebel, in Lockean theory, is not the majority who resist but rather the government, which has violated the trust.[33] Law is the will of the majority limited to the preservation of natural rights decreed by the social contract, or law is the way in which the majority chooses to secure natural rights. Political power and thus law are limited by the purposes for which they were created. Revolution, properly so-called, is the act and will of a majority of civil society. An individual rebel or a minority group of rebels are mere criminals.

WHAT IS THE CONSEQUENCE OF GIVING UP NATURAL RIGHTS?

Paradoxically, the consequence of giving up natural rights is the preservation of natural rights. One gives up his claim to everything in order to secure his claims to the most personally important things: to life, according to Hobbes; to life, liberty, and estate, according to Locke. An authority is created, a common judge is commissioned, a government is founded to protect inalienable natural rights. The paradox of natural rights is that they can be attained only through their loss, just as in the Christian tradition one must die to gain life eternal.

A further consequence of giving up natural rights is that

it creates a new definition of justice. Justice is simply keeping one's contracts.[34] Justice is keeping the social contract. Injustice is *injury where there is an obligation not to injure.* There is no obligation whatsoever in the state of nature, and so, while men may injure each other there, they cannot commit an act of injustice. Tragedy is one thing, injustice is another. In the state of nature, no moral distinction can be made between death, suffering, and harm at the hands of a man, and the same as the consequence of flood, fire, or hurricane. There is no difference, in the state of nature, between being killed by a tree branch driven by the wind and being killed by a man wielding a tree branch as a club. Each case is equally tragic, in each case a man is just as dead, and in each case the action is amoral. Man is, in the state of nature, simply another wild natural force. The only real distinction between man and the natural elements that can cause so much tragedy is that man has an independent will, and thus can promise to forbear. It is this promise that gives birth to justice and injustice.

Justice is legal simply because justice is created by men, by their freely given consent. It is not natural but conventional. This is of great significance because it appears to solve the dilemma of the universal and the particular that the ancient political philosophers believed to be a fundamentally intransigent problem. Justice, said Socrates, is a universal, and is superior to law, which is necessarily particular. Justice and law are not identical or are only identical in the best regime simply. There is in all actual regimes a conflict between the good man, the man who is just, and the good citizen, the man who obeys the law. The conflict cannot be resolved in favor of justice because only the wise know what justice is, and thus most men need law to live reasonably well. The rule of law, as Socrates taught in the *Crito,* is a very high thing, but it is not the highest thing.

The modern political philosophers made law the highest thing, and they did so by converting inalienable natural rights into sociopolitical rights. Once the social contract has been made, the highest claim a man can make is to that social contract, since all of his inalienable natural rights are incorporated into it. Inalienable natural rights are now the motive or cause for law, authorized by law, merged into law. The goal or end of the social contract is the preservation of natural rights, and so natural rights are now legal rights. In overcoming the defects of nature, men have invented justice by transforming natural rights into conventional rights, by exchanging contestable claims for incontestable claims.

Another consequence of giving up natural rights is that it apparently mitigates the tension between wisdom and consent, a problem the ancient philosophers also considered to be intractable. Good government, according to the ancients, required the rule or at least the input of the wise, those who can distinguish the real good from the apparent good, those who understand the purpose of human life, the terminal excellence of man. This kind of understanding comes only to a few rare men, men who are not usually recognized in their own time. Consent was necessary, the ancients thought, but only wisdom was sufficient title to rule.

The modern natural rights theory of Hobbes and Locke is not based on the development of the virtue wisdom, but rather on the passion for self-preservation. Civil society is created and governments are formed by the relatively simple act of voluntarily giving up some natural rights to make others more secure. Wisdom is not within the scope of all men, but consent, voluntary yielding of something that they already possess, is. Although reason plays a role in modern natural right theory, reason, as Hobbes and Locke defined it, bore little resemblance to wisdom. It was not man's link with the eternal order; it was merely calculation of self-interest. There is nothing noble about human reason so defined, but there is this obvious advantage: it is within the capacity of the meanest man. The ground of political life may be low, but it is solid.

Modern natural rights theory has, therefore, broadened the base of political life; it has widened and flattened out the foundation of government. The problems of the human condition can be solved not by developing human character and teaching men the ways of virtue; rather they can be solved by the construction of the proper institutions. Institutions and procedures become the instruments of human salvation. Human passion harnessed to the machinery of political institutions will insure progress. The polis, the political community, is not a way of life, a total environment in which human nature can flourish and flower; it is simply a device or contrivance—mere apparatus. Technique becomes everything and temperament becomes nothing.

Nature provides no model for ruling and being ruled, but man's reason, his calculation of his interest, has invented one. Man has improved upon nature; man has produced order out of disorder. Man has a nature that is natural rights but that, as it spontaneously manifests itself, is defective and can only be remedied by the active intervention of men themselves. In short, men by their own acts can perfect their own natures. The specific act required is the creation of the social contract or the foundation of a political organization. Civil society and government are the manmade remedies for the disease of nature.

ROUSSEAU'S DISSENT

The majority opinion, as articulated by Hobbes and Locke, is that the state of nature is a negative pole, a condition "not to be endured," and that man through his own effort and as an act of his will has solved the problem of nature. Jean-Jacques Rousseau, however, took another look at the social contract and came away with an entirely different opinion about its value. His grave doubts about civil society are reflected in his famous statement, "Man was born free and everywhere he is in chains."[35] His doubts about civil society are a direct product of his disagreement with Hobbes and Locke about the state of nature. His own analysis led him to conclude that the state of nature is a positive pole, a condition of contentment, and above all a state of perfect freedom.

According to Rousseau, men by nature are: radically asocial, living entirely alone; not rational, having no speech and no occasion to develop it because of their radical asociality; equal, though simply in physical existence since differences of body and talent are not observable and can have no discernable effects in a radically asocial life; and perfectible, adaptable, capable of adding things to themselves that can be retained from generation to generation.[36] All of this means, according to Rousseau, that man by nature is free, radically independent and undetermined. Natural freedom is the highest, the essential "right" or characteristic of man as man. It is what distinguished men from beasts.[37]

Hobbes and Locke had agreed that men left the state of nature by the process of relinquishing natural rights, which is actually a consent to duties. Rousseau agrees that men left the state of nature, and they did so by adding sociality to themselves or, more aptly, by becoming more and more dependent upon others.

On leaving the state of nature, men gradually lost more and more of their freedom as they became dependent upon one another for physical and psychological survival. The climax of this degeneration of human independence occurred when men made the social contract, because the social contract not only legitimizes inequalities, it also alienates men from their true selves, binding them to the will of others, defining their existence in terms of their relationships with others and their duties to others.[38] The social contract is a massive swindle in Rousseau's eyes because it legitimates dominance and maintains it by the public force.[39] A free man is self-determining, a free man rules himself, but under the social contract most if not all men are ruled, their lives are determined for them. Thus, Rousseau finds that men not only can give up natural rights but, contrary to Hobbes and Locke, men have given up the essential right— freedom. They gave up this right when they made the social contract, when they agreed to be ruled by others, by society, and by government.

The crisis of civilized man is acute because the obvious remedy, a return to the state of nature, is impossible.[40] The freedom of the state of nature was irrevocably lost when men added sociality to their natures. Natural freedom, doing whatever one likes, was possible when men were radically asocial. With almost no human intercourse, there would be almost no conflicts of freedom. Once men became social animals, the conflicts of natural freedom multiplied, and one man's freedom became another man's bondage. Men claimed the same things at the same time, and thus the conflict of natural freedom came to be. Men have changed, have added things to themselves that they now cannot do without. Men have added reason and sociality to their natures. Just as human life came from, evolved out of, the sea, so men have evolved out of the state of nature. Just as we cannot return to live in the sea, just as we have lost the natural ability to live an aquatic life, so have we lost the simple freedom of the state of nature. The crisis is acute. The solution, according to Rousseau, is to create an artificial freedom, just as we by artifice return to the sea in submarines and scuba gear.

The solution to this thoroughly modern problem, ironically, is a return to the ancient polis where there is no distinction between individual and society, where the political community is an organic whole. To be free again, every man must give himself entirely to the community of men.[41] Each gives himself to the whole and to no other individual or faction. The law of this community is the general will.[42] Each man participates in or wills the general will, and, therefore, the general will is his individual will.[43] The private person by an act of will converts himself into the citizen, and the citizen of an ancient polis is, according to Aristotle, a ruler, an office holder, a trustee. The citizen obeys the law, but the law is his will, and the man who obeys only his own will is free.

The distinction between a private person and a citizen is

crucial to Rousseau's understanding of the general will. He points out that as a private person a man can have a private, that is a selfish, will but as a citizen, he can only have a public or general will, as a citizen he can only will the common good.[44] Since a man's private or selfish interest may be (and often is) in conflict with the common good, it is possible, if not probable, that man-the-private-person will renege on his obligations as man-the-citizen, in order to obtain his selfish interest. Recalling that a man is free only because he voluntarily becomes a citizen, or only because he wills the general will, it follows that when society compels a man, who would otherwise renege, to obey the law, to follow the general will, it is merely compelling him to be free.[45]

While Rousseau's statement that a man can be forced to be free appears to be a contradiction in terms, it actually is not. The real contradiction exists in the man who would renege. A man is a soccer player because he chooses to play the game of soccer, because he agrees to abide by the rules of the game of soccer, rather than to do what is convenient or expedient for him at the moment. In soccer, no player except the goalie can touch the ball with his hands in bounds. To do so is to break the rules, but it is the rules that make a man a soccer player, as opposed to a basketball player, etc. Thus the referee and the other players are merely forcing a man to be what he himself chose to be—a soccer player—when they compel him not to use his hands. Because they compel him to keep his promise, to abide by the rules, they release him from the bonds of contradiction; they free him, so that he can be a soccer player.

Each man, in willing the general will, makes the laws that he will obey, and thus is self-determining. This is formal or artificial freedom, not natural freedom. It is, nonetheless, freedom, despite its formality. Rousseau takes the modern principle of consent and ennobles it. A man agrees not just to give up some of his natural rights, not just to give his executive proxy to society and government, not just to give up the right to use force; a man agrees to control himself, to discipline his desires, to restrain his passions. In short, he agrees to practice the virtues.[46]

Natural man had no virtues; he needed none. He was "good" in the negative sense of having no reason or occasion to do harm. It is true enough to say that a cow does not lie or steal, but it is as meaningless as to say it doesn't fly. Man in the state of nature does not lie or steal, and he doesn't fly either. In civil society, a social state, the private wills of men can and do conflict. The conflict, the conflict that Hobbes and Locke mistakenly called the state of nature, must be resolved by a social contract. The social contract will either be a harness for man's passions (in Rousseau's eyes a form of bondage) or it will be a hatchway through which men can escape compulsion and dominance.

To understand Rousseau's teaching on forms of government, one must keep in mind the distinction between the legislative and the executive functions. Under the social contract, the legislative form of government becomes all-important.[47] There is only one form of government, legislatively, that is conducive to artificial freedom, the simple participatory democracy. A man must have a direct hand in making all the laws; he must himself be a legislator. Therefore, the representative principle must be abandoned, and along with it, the large heterogeneous society.[48] The form of government in the executive sense may be either democratic, aristocratic or monarchical, but whatever the executive form, all public officers must be mere clerks or administrative officers who are given complete instructions. They can be permitted no discretion, no independent judgment.[49] Whenever there is a new problem, they must return for instructions to the legislature where every citizen represents himself.

The laws that are produced by the general will must look to the formation of character, the education of men in the virtues.[50] A man who corrupts himself corrupts a legislator and thus the law itself. Every man holds a public office, and a public office is a public trust. Trustees are held to the highest standard and so, therefore, is each man. This is a free society because its people are simple and virtuous.

Although Rousseau's solution is a return to ancient practice, he is a modern political philosopher because his principles are modern. He, along with Hobbes and Locke, looks to the raw and primitive beginnings not to the final goal of human life for his political standard. He denies the sociopolitical nature of man and finds that government is a construct. He agrees that there is no natural authority and no natural title to rule. He bases government entirely on consent not on wisdom, and his highest value is freedom not virtue. Virtue in Rousseau's theory is utilitarian; it is the only means available for regaining our lost natural freedom. Thus, he turns the ancient theory upside down. The ancient political philosophers agreed that man is free, but they asked, What is freedom for? Their answer, Freedom is for virtue, and virtue is the highest thing, the purpose of human life, is in stark contrast with Rousseau's principle that freedom is the end and virtue merely the means.

Nature provides no models for ruling, but it does provide the model for happiness. The natural model, however, has not only been redefined but also irrevocably destroyed. Human happiness, which is freedom, now depends entirely upon art. Nature, the politically definitive criterion in ancient thought, has been reduced, redefined, and largely replaced. The remnant contribution of nature to human life is so small that the concept of nature has, in Rousseau's theory, almost no political significance.

Chapter 8

THE CROSSCURRENT

Past and to come seem best; things present worst.
                                                            Shakespeare

The concept of nature, the concept of the essential, given, constant characteristics of a being called man, served as the standard for political philosophers of the mainstream, both ancient and modern, for two thousand years. By the middle of the nineteenth century, however, a crosscurrent had developed with sufficient force to challenge the basic premise of the mainstream. This crosscurrent is defined by its rejection of nature as a standard for political things, and, most importantly, by its implicit denial that there is such a thing as human nature. If there is no such thing as human nature, it cannot serve as a standard for evaluating political things nor can it serve as a basis for political prescription. Indeed, the fundamental principles of the crosscurrent make politics irrelevant, a dinosaur, a curiosity, an object of interest only to dusty antiquarians.

According to the crosscurrent, neither politics nor man is a natural phenomenon. The two major figures of the crosscurrent, Marx and Nietzsche, are diametrically opposed to each other on a number of basic issues. They disagree about the significance, character and power of history, economics, culture, and the human will. They are, in many respects, polar opposites. There is one basic and overriding point on which they agree: Man is not a being, he is a becoming; he is a growth without a terminus, a creature whose qualities are neither permanent, settled nor ascertainable. There are no natural rights or freedoms that exist in a state of nature and that cannot be alienated. Natural-rights theory is a theory based on certain fixed characteristics, unchangeable properties that man possesses by virtue of being a man. There is no natural justice that is the proper function and the highest goal of human life. Natural justice theory is a theory based on certain fixed qualities, unchangeable excellences that man is designed to pursue by virtue of being a man.

Natural rights and natural justice are not valid premises for political philosophy because they are deductions from statements about man that are assumed to be enduring truths, resistant to both time and change. The crosscurrent contends that natural rights and natural justice are not valid premises for political philosophy because nothing is resistant to time and change; there is no enduring truth except the truth of impermanence. If this is so, there can be no true science of man, no political science in the traditional sense that, on the basis of timeless truths about man, predicts and prescribes for human behavior. There can only be a science of history, an account of the change and motion, development and destruction.

Political science, as practiced by the philosophers of the mainstream, construes human nature and infers from it principles of government appropriate to the security of natural rights or the achievement of natural justice. It assumes that a political-anthropology is controlling and that principles of government can be deduced from human nature. The mainstream asks, What is man? Are political things natural to man? Who should rule? What are the proper goals of ruling? What limits should be placed on ruling? What is the proper relationship between the individual and the organized group?

According to the crosscurrent, human nature cannot be construed because it is continuously changing. Principles of government cannot be deduced from human nature because human nature is relative to time, place, and circumstance. Politics is not the architectonic discipline; it is dependent and controlled by outside forces whether economic-historic or cultural-psychological. The crosscurrent asks, What kinds of men have there been? What kinds of men are now? What historical or economic forces shaped the men of a given time? What cultural or psychological forces molded men of a given place? What destroyed these forces and what replaced them? What forces shape human life in our time? The crosscurrent does not prescribe either a way of life or a form of government because it has no basis for prescription, it has no standard, no settled, final concept of what man *should* be or become. As to what man *will* become, the crosscurrent merely speculates, noting that prediction is impossible regarding the radically creative creature man.

MARX

Karl Marx, the most influential philosopher of the crosscurrent, perceived man as an animal who is ultimately his own creator. According to Marx, man is the producing animal.[1] He creates not only productive forces such as plows and tractors, not only modes of production such as feudalism and capitalism, but he creates history, and in so doing, he changes from epoch to epoch, ultimately creating his own essence, his own "nature."[2] This essence or "nature," however, is not limited in any way. This final accomplishment of man is not a terminal excellence as the ancient philosophers would have understood it. It is not a limitation on being, however admirable or desirable it may be. It is, rather, a complete release of man's creativity from the dynamics of class struggle; it is the end of history, the end of limitation, the end of restraint, the attainment of freedom simply.

As an animal, man requires certain material things (food, shelter, etc.) to maintain his being. To survive, he must either find these things or produce them. The means by which his material necessities are produced are called the productive forces, and these productive forces are created by men. Thus, men domesticate animals or invent the plow. These productive forces must be arranged and ordered in a general manner or method of production (feudalism, capitalism) that Marx calls a mode of production. However, there is only one mode of production appropriate to or that conforms with a given set of productive forces. Thus, the productive forces available at any given time determine the mode of production. The steam engine does not conform to a feudal mode but rather to a capitalistic one. When new productive forces become available, the mode of production changes.

Further, for every given mode of production there corresponds one and only one kind of social life and social organization. The personal reciprocal relationships, the old ties of family and of fief, of birth and of land, do not conform to the capitalistic mode of production and cannot long survive the introduction of capitalism. Since men create the productive forces that lend themselves to only one mode of production, that in turn goes with only one form of society, men, in creating modes of production are unconsciously creating a total environment, a complete way of life and thought. Everything is derivative of the initial and basic productive act. There is a kind of ripple effect in which a culture or way of life is merely the largest circle in a series of circles begun when a rock is dropped into a pond. The consequences of these basic and primary productive acts are enormous for they set in motion a process that will culminate in a new type of human being, a being who has formed himself through his own labor.

In history, whatever man is, is what he has made of himself. But, even in history, according to Marx, we cannot use the term man without placing a restricting adjective before it.[3] The term man implies a human nature that is unchanging, that cuts across time and place. Man does not simply add things to his nature (as Rousseau contended) expanding its scope with social needs, rather he completely alters his "nature." Thus, there was feudal man, and capitalistic man, but no such thing as man simply, a being with an ascertainable, universal nature. Feudal man and capitalistic man are as different as two distinct species, as different as the fox and the lion. Each is of his own historic time and place. Each is the captive of his historic time and place and can no more transcend or rise above that way of being than the fox can adopt the way of being of the lion. Everything that feudal man is, his very thoughts, his way of perceiving and evaluating his social, political, cultural environment are determined by his historic time and place, which are in turn determined by the modes of production man himself has created.[4] While the philosophers of the mainstream all agreed that some men could discover the truth about man, Marx argues that there is no truth that is not relative to one's historic time and place, relative to the prevailing mode of production.

Man creates modes of production and the modes of production make men what they are in history.[5] Men created these modes of production out of economic need, not as a result of a freely operating creative will. Men do not choose a particular form of government or of society in the sense that they pick the form monarchy or democracy. Rather, men create productive forces, and the specific kind of productive forces in turn establish a mode or method of production, which in turn establishes an entire sociopolitical structure. Therefore, men who have invented the productive force grazing animals, men who have domesticated animals and who live off of their meat and milk and hides will become nomads because the herds must continually move on to new grazing grounds. A whole nomadic sociopolitical structure follows from this. When men invent agriculture, when they invent the plow and live off of the harvest, they must give up their nomadic ways and become sedentary. Their entire sociopolitical life adapts itself to the necessities of agriculture.

Through time, each mode of production spontaneously

generates its own antithesis. This occurs because under each historic mode of production some men own the land and others merely labor on the land of the owners. Those who do not own the means of production are dependent upon those who do, and so distinct classes are created in each historic time, the class of owners and the various classes of nonowner laborers. The owners define the tasks that will be performed by each nonowner, and they organize the labor of the nonowners. In this division of labor, a man becomes alienated from himself, is defined by his assigned task, and relates to others in terms of his assigned task.[6] The whole multifaceted man is lost both to himself and to others in the division of labor, and his identity is reduced to the performance of a specialized task. Thus, a carpenter is the labor in my table, and a lumberjack is the labor in the wood the carpenter uses to make my table. The true community of men dissolves as it divides into distinct privatized groups—into butchers, bakers, and candlestick makers, whose interests diverge and conflict. The clash of interests is constrained by the state as controlled by the dominant class of owners.

The creation of distinct classes on the basis of the ownership of the means of production and the division of labor yields not only alienation and class conflict, but also revolution.[7] The contradictions between the dominant class and the dependent and oppressed classes eventually and inevitably generate a revolution, for the contradictions are so fundamental that compromises must fail. Like oil and water, they will not mix without the emulsifying turbulence of revolution. Class conflict, in the form of revolutionary annihilation of the existing ruling economic class by a newly emerging one, is, according to Marx, a universal law of motion, the motion Marx calls history.[8] Conflict, contradiction, and negation, in a word (the word most commonly associated with Marx) revolution, are not temporary aberrations; they are the essence of the process of development Marx calls history.[9]

Despite alienation and class conflict, there is no moral opprobrium to be attached to the owners, for they are as much caught up in their historic time and place as are the nonowners. They literally cannot be other than they are; they cannot do other than they do. They are what they are because of the prevailing mode of production in their time and not because they freely chose to be what they are.[10] The situation is a paradox: Men are at once the producers of their historic milieu and are produced by it.

One historic epoch succeeds another because the conflict between the owners of one means of production and the nonowners generates needs, which in turn provoke the creative forces in men who invent a new mode of production.[11] The new mode eventually replaces the old one, and this conflict of modes of production or of historic epochs recurs until but two classes remain, the capitalist class and the proletariat. In destroying the capitalist class, the proletariat-laboring class creates one class, or destroys the concept of class conflict.[12] If there remains but one class there can be no conflict of classes. At this point, history will end because history is class conflict. At this point, men will have completed the historic process of making their own "natures," and man's radical creativity will be released from the bonds of history.

What man will be at this point cannot be defined positively but only negatively, for man's creativity will be completely liberated, and there is no rational way to predict or even to prophesy radical creativity. To do so would be to place limits on man, and that is diametrically opposed to the concept of radical creativity. All that we can safely say about man in this posthistorical period is what he will not be.[13] He will not be as he was in history—political. In the posthistorical period there will not and cannot be government of any kind in the basic sense of ruling and being ruled, of one class of men commanding another. Whatever form of social organization obtains then, and Marx does not presume to describe it, it will not be government.

The truth about man, according to Marx, is that he is an evergrowing reed, that he is an evolving, changing animal whose growth does not have a terminus. In history, man's destiny is the end of history, but once this point is reached, man breaks through to a new dimension, a new way of becoming, a way that cannot be understood or known because it is not fixed, and it is never finished. The end of history, according to Marx, is the end of alienation and of class conflict, but it is also the end of political life and of political philosophy.

NIETZSCHE

Like Marx, Nietzsche emphatically rejects the mainstream's theory of human nature as the central political philosophic standard. Man's "nature," said Nietzsche, is to have no nature.[14] However, he just as emphatically rejects the historical process as a replacement for a theory of human nature.[15] History, as Marx understood it, is rational and purposive. It has a goal—its own termination, which when fully achieved is coeval with freedom. History is eventually meaningful; historic man has a destiny. The purposes of history cannot be understood until it is almost over. Marx claims to understand history and to accurately predict its outcome only because the end is nearly at hand; as one can accurately predict the outcome of a horse race as the leading horse reaches for the wire.

Despite its implicit attack on the mainstream's theory of human nature, Nietzsche finds that the rational-historical process theory is just as false and as deadly. Further, it is subject to the same errors. Marx spurned the purposiveness and the rationality of nature that Socrates had made the foundation stone of Western political thought. In its place, however, he set a rational and purposive historical process. Nietzsche rejects both theories on the same ground. Neither nature nor history are rational and purposive. The world is a chaos not a cosmos.[16] Paraphrasing Shakespeare's Macbeth, he would find that history is "a tale told by an idiot, full of sound and fury, signifying nothing." Paraphrasing Matthew Arnold, he would find that

nature is "a darkling plain swept with confused alarms of struggle and flight where ignorant armies clash by night." Since the
universe is a chaos, it has no design, it admits of no mission,
it moves without direction. Aimless and meaningless, it is unknown and unknowable.

Because men live in and are part of a fundamental chaos,
human life is not and cannot be a state of becoming that seeks
being, that seeks completion and perfection. Human life is simply an eternal becoming. Life has no purpose, no rhyme and
reason, no why and wherefore. Life is for itself; it is its own
purpose; it is not for something else.[17] Life is simply energy
releasing itself, letting off steam. There is no natural terminal
excellence for men to seek. There is no historical zenith. There
are no limitations on man, no boundaries and barriers that
cannot be overcome by human creativity or will. Neither nature
nor history can confine human will in their neat little boxes of
rationality and purpose. Human life cannot be understood; it
can only be experienced and dissipated, can only be lived.

To live well, or to use Nietzschean terminology, to live
healthily and energetically, men must live within a cultural
horizon.[18] A horizon is boundary. It is the place where earth
and sky meet. It is the place where a man will fall into the
swirling blackness if he steps forward. A cultural horizon is a
boundary. It is a set of assumptions about what is good and true
and beautiful, assumptions about God, the nature of man and
man's purpose in the universe. It limits and directs choices.[19]
It tells us metaphorically, "Go to Oz! Follow the yellow brick
road." It gives activity a purpose. It tells us where and how and
to what end to release our living energy. To live without a
horizon is to stand at a crossroads with no signposts, no map,
no guidebook, no sense of direction, and no destination. Too
many choices and no way to evaluate them bewilder and ultimately paralyze. A cultural horizon is a way of looking at the
world that structures experience and makes it manageable by
blocking out incompatibilities. All cultural horizons are false;
they are at best noble myths.

Since cultural horizons are necessary for the healthy, energy-releasing life, they are good though untrue. The good life, that is the active, striving, struggling life, is incompatible with truth. The truth is that nothing is true, and the truth is deadly.[20] The universe is characterized by the utmost meaninglessness. The world is not an orderly harmonious system; it is utter disorder and confusion. The truth is that all cultural horizons are arbitrary. Once this truth is known, God is dead, and men become contemptible. The men who know the truth are the last men, the men without aspiration, without longing, without dedication.[21] The last men have nothing to do, for there is nothing to do. Without goals, men become passive rather than active. This is aptly called the old age of mankind, the time the mind and the spirit deteriorate faster than the body, when men die merely because they have no will, no reason to live, the listless time, the time of fatiguing inactivity, of wearying uselessness. Such men live the lives of grazing herbivores, insipid, tame, and uninteresting. Truth is a fatal disease; it is totally destructive of life, that thrusting, demanding assertion of power and will.

Within the mainstream, the ancients had recognized that most men live within cultural horizons that are semimythical or at least particular, and that such horizons are necessary because of the limited ability of most men to transcend the realm of opinion to the realm of knowledge. Plato's famous allegory of the cave illustrates this point as well as the fundamental difference between Nietzsche and the mainstream. Plato had described all men as in a cave, chained together so that they must face the interior wall.[22] Everything they see is a shadow on the wall of the cave. Since they see only shadows, they assume that these shadows are the real things. One day, one man breaks his chains and turns and goes out of the cave. There he sees the sun; he sees real things not shadows. This man, according to Plato, is the happiest of all men for he perceives the truth and beauty of the cosmos. Nietzsche agrees with Plato that it is possible to break the chains and leave the cave, but when a man does so he does not see the sun because there is no sun. There is nothing but an abyss, a swirling blackness. There is nothing to give impetus to action. This man is a man of the utmost despair. The healthy men, the vigorous men are the men in the cave.

If the universe is a chaos, truth is in conflict with life because truth destroys cultural horizons, which are necessary for the activity called life, for the dissipation of the energy that is creativity. In such a conflict, life is to be preferred to truth.[23] The rub is that once the truth is known, it is impossible to unknow it. To say, God is dead but because it makes me feel better I'll pretend that he is alive and well and living in Mexico, is contemptible. We cannot act on the reality of illusions once we recognize that they are illusions.

The only solution to the modern crisis that Nietzsche offers is the merest possibility of the superman, who could be produced by the will to power.[24] Man, said Nietzsche, wills all things. Living is willing; it is overcoming, striving, and mastering. In the past, man has created cultural horizons by unconsciously imposing his will on the world and arbitrarily imposing an order and meaning where there was no order and meaning. The great founders, Theseus, Romulus, and the rare men of their ilk, were horizon builders. They created great cultures by the sheer force of their unconscious, overcoming wills. Believing that they merely revealed the will of the gods or the eternal and unchanging truths, they in fact and unaware imposed their own wills, their own choices, and thereby built a fortress of invigorating ideas within which their followers could live healthy purposeful active lives. If all things can be willed, if everything can be overcome by the release of living energy, then perhaps the superman can be willed.[25] If so, for the first time a man could consciously create a horizon; if so, human creativity would become conscious of its power; the most radical, the most plenary human creativity of all would be cognizant of itself and its vigor. If nothing is true, everything is possible, everything can be overcome, mastered; everything can be willed. Nietzsche's superman wills himself because he wills not only his future but his past, and thereby assumes the most awesome responsibility for himself and his actions. Perhaps the superman can be willed, perhaps, but if not the old age of mankind has been reached, and there is nothing left but the last men.

No political solution, no political program or prescription can produce the superman and resolve the crisis of our time, can revitalize the decadent last men. The crosscurrent not only denies a human nature but it is inherently apolitical. Neither Marx nor Nietzsche offers political prescriptions properly. Neither takes his bearings from ruling and being ruled. Marx looks to economics and to a rational historic process to provide the ultimate solutions to the fundamental problems of human life. Nietzsche, whose tragic view of human life persists, offers the merest possibility of a solution in a psychology of demoniac will.

Forms of government, administrative framework, the common judge, the rule of law, the reciprocity of rights and duties, and the authority of human reason, these basic ingredients of the political process are irrelevant. They are illusions and ideology. The crosscurrent dethrones politics as the queen of the social sciences. It debunks the energizing principle of politics—the nature of man. Its hero is not the citizen, the man whose dignity derives from the fact that he participates in ruling, but is, rather, the artist, the radically creative man whose spontaneity is unrestrained by rules.

The crosscurrent is part of the tradition we call Western political philosophy because it addresses the same fundamental questions: What is man? What is the best way for a man to live? How can men best live together? It is part of the tradition because it also shares the mainstream's understanding of the evaluative and analytic tasks of the political philosopher. The crosscurrent, too, perceives the role of the political philosopher to be a diagnostician of the human condition. It is a crosscurrent, however, because its answers to the fundamental questions contradict the elemental principles of the mainstream. It answers, Man is not a being, he is a becoming; man does not have a nature; he should live energetically, spontaneously, and apolitically. It is a crosscurrent because its "prescriptions" are ultimately not prescriptions properly (and especially not political prescriptions), but rather, predictions of either the end of economic class conflict and history, or the end of man as we have known him.

Chapter 9

THE PRINCIPLES OF THE MAINSTREAM OF WESTERN POLITICAL THOUGHT

Man is the only animal that laughs and weeps; for he is the only animal that is struck with the difference between what things are, and what they ought to be.

William Hazlitt

In what is perhaps the most concise description of political philosophy ever made, Henry Adams wrote, "Knowledge of human nature is the beginning and end of a political education." What is man's nature? What is man for? What is the good for man as man? How shall I live? How shall men live together?

Whatever its formulation, the fundamental question of the mainstream of Western political philosophy is, What is man? Every political philosophy in this tradition is grounded on an answer to this basic question. From Aristotle, who proclaimed that man is the political animal, to Rousseau, who declared that man was born free, political philosophers of the mainstream have based their evaluations and prescriptions on a theory of human nature.

Politics is the art of human government or the science of the common affairs of men, and thus the nature of man is the appropriate standard for these human activities. Government is a rule and a measure, and every rule and measure must be homogeneous with what it rules and measures. But the preoccupation with the nature of man is as much a celebration or solemnization of man as a concern for an appropriate and accurate standard of measurement. Human beings have long taken themselves seriously, have long considered themselves a special or unique phenomenon. The political philosophers of the Western tradition are no exception. They have seen man as possessing a distinguished or higher rank in the natural order, or they have seen man as being in nature, though not necessarily of it. Whatever their final definitions of the nature of man, however they have differed in their definitions of man's nature, they have all agreed that man's is not just one nature among many, not just one animal among many, but that there is something out of the ordinary about the nature of man, something notable and remarkable. The coherence of the tradition we call Western political philosophy begins with the simple principle that man is a unique animal.

The mainstream of Western political philosophy has two tributaries. The distinguishing mark of each tributary is its position on the naturalness of political things or its position on the political nature of man. Although the ancients and the moderns take diametrically opposed positions on this basic principle, they converge on the value, on the desirability of political life. The mainstream of Western political philosophy is explicitly antianarchical and propolitical.

The ancients staunchly maintained that man is a political animal by nature. The moderns as vehemently contended that man is a political animal by convention or art. The quarrels between the two groups over the source of government are so obvious and produce such a variety of political prescription that we tend to forget what is common to both: the primacy and dignity of politics as an attribute of man.

Whether nature, which does nothing in vain, has fixed politics as a human attribute, or whether man, recognizing the defects of nature, has invented politics and added it to himself, the mainstream of Western political thought agrees that political life is purposive. The purpose may be delivery from an unendurable condition, as in modern thought, or it may be achievement of a terminal excellence, as in ancient thought, but in either case politics is an instrumental end and not a final end. It is a means or agency of something higher than itself. It is a means of human happiness. Thus, political philosophers of the mainstream study the nature of man not only to elaborate a standard for evaluating political things, but also they evaluate political things in order to prescribe remedies for political defects; thereby to actualize, to secure man's uncommon place among the phenomena of nature.

THE FUNDAMENTAL PROBLEM OF POLITICS

The properly constituted polity, according to both the ancients and the moderns, is one directed toward the common good, and the common good for both groups of philosophers is the well-being of man as man, his happiness or the conditions thereof. The philosophers of the mainstream not only agree that political life is purposive, and that its purpose is human happiness, but they also agree that its purpose is *individual* happiness. The association of the many, whether by nature or by convention, is ultimately for the individual as individual. The political community exists for man rather than man for the political community.

This theorem is reflected in the resolutions both groups offer to the fundamental problem of politics, the problem of the one and the many. The problem of the one and the many refers to the conflicts that arise between a man and his polity, between the individual and the community. The problem is fundamental and seemingly intransigent because it is an ethical dilemma. It is a problem that requires a choice between desirable but apparently contradictory goods, the individual or personal good of a man as a single entity and the good of the community as community.

On the most elemental level, the level upon which modern

thought tends to focus, there is a disharmony or conflict between the common good, defined as the life of the regime, and the personal good, the most basic natural right, the life of the individual. Every political community at some time or other of necessity demands of its citizens that they risk their own lives in defense of that community. Life is the *sine qua non* of all individual human happiness. Logically, in order to be happy one must first be. Nonetheless, the life of the political community is also indispensable to individual happiness since it serves as the common judge and reduces the use of force without right.

On the highest level, the level upon which ancient thought tends to focus, there is or can be a clear conflict between the common good, defined as the rule of law, and the personal good, the terminal excellence of man, the virtuous life. This conflict, the conflict between the good citizen and the good man, exemplified in the trial and conviction of Socrates, arises because no community's laws are simply just. The laws of every polity are to a large extent particular, for this time, this place, these people, and these conditions, but the good is universal, it is always and everywhere the same. The good citizen is the man who obeys the laws of his polity, but the good man is virtuous. Since law and virtue, or law and justice, are not simply identical, the individual good and the common good may not be identical or there is a potential incongruity between the good citizen and the good man.

The political problem, then, is how to reconcile this conflict between the individual and the group. On the resolution, the ancients and the moderns differ because they disagree about the concept of nature and the naturalness of political things. For the ancients the ultimate resolution occurs only in the best regime simply, or it occurs only in the most natural regime. In the best regime simply, the good man can be a good citizen because in this regime the wise, those who know what justice is, rule. This resolution is based on something that is not only natural, but that is most natural, because it is higher than political life, it is based on the philosophic life. For the moderns, the resolution is initially the social contract, a product of the freedom of the individual will actively, rationally, and consciously creating or positing duties in order to secure rights. The ultimate development of this modern resolution is found not in the best regime simply but in Rousseau's general will theory. This resolution is based on something that is not only conventional but that is radically and stringently conventional, it is based on a calculated alienation of natural rights.

According to ancient thought, the resolution of the problem of the one and the many turns on the wisdom or virtue of the individual. The common good is eminent, but it is not preeminent, it does not override the privilege conferred by wisdom. As Socrates teaches in the *Apology* and the *Crito,* a man should be willing to give up his life for his polity, freely and with dignity, but a man must never abandon the pursuit of excellence.

According to modern thought, the resolution of the problem of the one and the many turns on the inalienability of some natural rights. A man must keep his freely given promises, he must perform his covenants. The common good is eminent, but it is not preeminent, it does not override a man's prepolitical inalienable rights. A man must abide by the decision of the common judge whenever it is present, but when it is not or when it usurps the trust and exercises powers not delegated to it, he must himself vindicate his natural rights.

A common theme in both these resolutions is the superiority of the individual, or the good of the individual is the final end of politics, whether politics be natural or conventional. The good man is the final measure of all regimes, according to the ancients, and the best test of any regime is the kind of men it produces. Politics is a natural process. The political community is a very high thing because there and there alone can a man develop his full natural potential. The common good, the proper goal of the political community, is a very high thing, but it is not the highest thing. Man ultimately transcends the political community because in his consummation he can achieve a level of excellence beyond that of even the good political community. Aristotle, in the middle of his argument for the rule of the people, the argument based on the collective wisdom of the people, reminds us that collective wisdom notwithstanding there is no substitute for the wisdom of *a* good man. The good man has no political equivalent; the good man can philosophize and the political community cannot; the good man can pursue excellence simply and the political community cannot. The political community is limited to the excellence achievable by most men, not to the excellence achievable by the best man.

Although they dropped the qualifying adjective "good" from the ancient's formulation of the problem, the good man vs. the good citizen, and thereby reduced both man and the political community, the moderns retained the concept of man as the measure of all things political. They substituted the rights of man for the concept of the good man as the best test of any regime. The final measure of any political community is the secured rights of men. Politics is a conventional process. The political community is a very high thing because it secures the rights of men, natural rights, which paradoxically are not secured by nature. The common good, the proper goal of the political community, is a very high thing, but it is not the highest thing. Man transcends the political community because the rights of man are prepolitical and independent of politics. Man transcends the political community because he is its creator, and the creator is superior to the creation. What a man can make he can change, he can unmake, he can destroy. Political things are subordinate to their source—man. Individual man has no political equivalent; man possesses absolute rights and the political community does not.

Although there is something higher than politics, and the mainstream of Western political philosophy is agreed on what is higher, man, though not on why, it also concurs on the worth and desirability of the political community and the rule of law, though again not on why.

According to ancient theory the political community is a

very high thing because it is natural. It is natural because it is necessary, or men can live well only in association with their fellows, and it is natural because it is the highest association, the most inclusive, the most self-sufficient association. All associations are established for some good. Since the political community is the most inclusive association, its goal is the most inclusive human good or the good life. Only the wise know what this good actually is, and therefore the political community is most properly directed by the wise. Unfortunately, they are rarely among us, and even when they are, their rule is not feasible without the consent of the many who are strong but not wise. Reason is a kind of power, but physical strength is a kind of reason. The wise who exercise the power of reason confront the many who evince the reason of power.

Since the wise are rarely among us, there must be a substitute for the rule of the wise; and since physical strength is an ultimate phenomenon, there must be an accommodation to the power of the many. The name of the substitute and the accommodation is the rule of law. The rule of law is the compromise between the wisdom of the few and the power of the many. The rule of law is a combination of the qualities of two different things, wisdom and strength (in numbers) one of which is contributory and subordinate to the other. The rule of law is a support that strength in numbers (consent) provides to the reason or to wisdom. The principles of law are formulated by the statesman and are informed by his reason rather than produced by his will. They are adopted by the many, becoming authoritative or achieving the status of law as an act of the will of the people. They become law not because they are principles of reason, but rather because they are posited by the many. What the many posit or authorize is good law to the extent that the rules are reasonable or that they reflect knowledge of the good for man as man. The rule of law is a very high thing because it is necessary. No association of men (not even a band of robbers) can exist without principles directing the conduct and guiding the interactions of the members. The rule of law is a very high thing because it is the vehicle through which wisdom can rule, or law can be (though not necessarily is) just. It is not, however, and it cannot be the highest thing because the rule of law is merely a substitute for and not an equivalent of the wisdom of the good man.

According to modern theory, the political community is a very high thing because it is unnatural. It is unnatural because it is a remedy for a natural defect. Men can live long only by device and strategem. It is unnatural because it is an association and a solemn covenant. In the state of nature men are asocial. All associations are conventional, the product of men's freely operating individual wills. In willing to leave the state of nature, men create an association that is superior to nature, or that represents an improvement upon and subjugation of nature. Nature is a total conflict of equal rights. There is no natural title to rule, and there are no natural rulers. Thus, there are no natural subjects and no natural obligations. Since nature does not supply a ruling principle, and since without one, life is unendurable, one must be constructed. The name of the ruling principle is the rule of law, and it is created by the freely consenting wills of men in a form called the social contract.

The rule of law is at once a conquest of nature and a confession of the natural vulnerability of men. The principles are formulated by a "studier" who rationally calculates that his personal advantage and everyone else's is general peace and prosperity. They are adopted or willed by each individual as individual, becoming authoritative or achieving the status of law precisely because they are rational, because they promote personal advantage. The rule of law is thus the combination of two powers, the reason and the will, one of which is ancillary and subordinate to the other. The rule of law is a service reason provides to the will or to the passions. These principles become law because they are reasonable, and they are good to the extent that they are reasonable, to the extent that they satisfy the passion for self-preservation, the passion for the protection of property in its largest sense of life, liberty, and estate.

The rule of law is a very high thing because it is expedient. It is the most prudent and sensible means of satisfying one's private passions, given the circumstances of a natural equality of right. The rule of law is a very high thing because it is the liberation of man from the conflict in nature. It is not, however, and cannot be the highest thing because it is a product of man's will to personal advantage and is limited by the purposes for which it was willed. It is not the highest thing because it is a remedy for and not an equivalent of natural rights.

THE FUNDAMENTAL AGREEMENT

As a result of the high value placed on the political community and the rule of law, the mainstream of Western political philosophy is not only explicitly antianarchical, but also implicitly dutiful. In short, the mainstream of the Western tradition postulates a general duty to obey the law. Law-abidingness for both the ancients and the moderns is essential, indispensable, and absolutely necessary. It is difficult to overemphasize this point in our time, because of all of the principles of the mainstream of Western thought, this is the most overloooked, the most forgotten, despite the fact that this is the point of fundamental agreement.

The art of politics is the art of ruling. The fundamental problem of politics, the problem of the one and the many, finds its *political* resolution in the act of ruling. The resolution of ancient thought, the best regime simply, is a political resolution because in it wisdom *rules,* the good man rules himself. The resolution of the moderns, the social contract, is a political resolution because under it men agree to control or *rule* themselves. Political man, or the man who rules, is called either the citizen or the tyrant. The tyrant rules alone. He may be supported or assisted by individuals or groups such as an army, but he does not share the ultimate authority. Tyranny is a regime composed of subjects. All other regimes whether good or bad in the ethical sense are composed of citizens, persons, whether the few or the many, whether rich or poor, who share authority and thereby rule themselves.

As Aristotle taught so long ago, to be a citizen is to hold a public office. A public office is a public trust, and a trustee not only has duties, but he is held to the highest standard of performance. Within any regime, persons, as opposed to citizens, have duties as well as rights, but the citizen by virtue of the fact that he holds an office, an office for which aliens and slaves are not eligible, has the highest duty to be law-abiding. As a citizen he is a ruler, he participates in the formation and the administration of the laws, and therefore, is self-determining, self-governing. Aristotle defined a citizen as a person who shares in the legislative-deliberative and the judicial-administrative functions of the polity. As the citizen has more duties and higher duties than a mere person, he has more rights and receives more benefits from the polity, for according to ancient thought rights and duties are reciprocal. One's rights are determined by one's duties, and one's duties by one's rights.

Citizenship is, as Aristotle pointed out, relative to the regime. It is the regime or constitution that determines who is and who is not a citizen; and so a man can be a citizen under one form of government or under one conception of justice and not under another. Nonetheless, whoever is a citizen under any given form of government is a ruler, and the good citizen is the one who performs his proper function; the good citizen is law-abiding.

While ancient thought traces citizenship to the regime, or to the form of government, modern thought traces citizenship to the social contract. Thus, a citizen is a person who makes the contract directly or tacitly. The social contract is a mutual pact and a form of shared responsibility. As a result of making this pact, men have claims upon each other, duties as well as rights. Once in civil society the term "right" is given substance; I have rights because you have duties and vice versa. The law of the social contract and all the lesser laws, which are derived from and consonant with it, define the rights and duties of citizens, those who are parties to the contract. In making the contract itself, each person literally participates in the legislative function, making not only the first real law, but the highest law, the law of laws, the law that governs all lesser laws. Therefore, the citizen is self-governing and self-determining. Furthermore, in making the social contract each person is making civil society, which exercises the judicial function. As a member of civil society, the individual participates in the judicial function, for, as Locke argued, it is civil society that collectively judges whether its agent, government, has usurped its function, whether its agent, government, has broken the law of the contract.

Although the moderns are divided on the significance of the form of the regime, that is, whether the form of government is determinative of citizenship, they are not divided on the principle of citizenship itself. Locke may have thought that only fools contest over forms of government, and Rousseau may have thought that only one form, a simple participatory democracy, was compatible with the concept of citizenship, but they agreed that the citizen is self-governing, that he is the original legislator, that he participates in the legislative and the judicial functions. The citizen is therefore a ruler, and the good citizen, the man who performs his contracts, is law-abiding. Citizens are not merely those who possess membership in a given political community, they are partners in self-determination, united and associated in the act of ruling.

Because, for both the ancients and the moderns, citizenship is a form of ruling and specifically it is self-rule, obedience to law is intrinsic to the idea of the citizen. A person who cannot participate in the legislative and judicial functions is not a citizen. Similarly, a person who does not obey the laws he has participated in making is not ruling himself and is, therefore, not a citizen in the proper sense. Those who are self-governing are free. Men can lose freedom in two ways. First, it can be taken from them, in Lockean terms, by an act of usurpation or, in Aristotelean terms, by a revolution or change of regime, a change that makes them ineligible for the office of citizen, as a change from a democracy to an oligarchy. Second, they can lose it by default, by a failure to exercise it, by a refusal to control themselves. This may be explained by analogy. In the midst of a family gathering, one child throws a tantrum screaming and kicking the floor, disturbing the whole assembled group. The parent physically removes the child, placing him in another room and ordering him to stay there until he can control himself. In this example, the parent clearly is ruling the child by force—by superiority of physical strength. Those who are ruled by force are subjects not citizens; they are not free. The issue is, why is the child so ruled, why is he not free? The answer is that he defaulted his freedom or refused to rule himself. Those who do not rule themselves make it necessary for others to rule them. In political terms, men must either rule or be ruled, they must either be citizens or subjects.

The mainstream of Western political thought thus identifies law-abidingness as a primary duty of citizenship, primary in the sense of being first in importance, and in the sense of being elemental or constituting a rudiment of citizenship. Law-abidingness is primary, but it is not absolute. The conditions under which the exceptions arise are, however, very narrow for both the ancients and the moderns.

For the ancients, the only exception to the general duty to obey the law is the privilege conferred by wisdom and maintained by prudence. This is an individual privilege, but since only a rare few are wise, it is not a privilege that the vast majority of men can ever rightfully claim. Only those who are actually wise may rightfully claim the privilege, and even this will not as a practical matter suffice, as the case of Socrates demonstrates. Socrates, of course, claimed that (according to his interpretation of the Delphic Oracle) he was the wisest man. He was, nonetheless, convicted of treason (corrupting the youth, the future rulers of a democracy) and executed. In neither the *Apology* nor the *Crito* does Socrates argue either that the laws he is charged with breaking are simply unjust or that he is simply innocent. In point of fact, Socrates is guilty, and he clearly knows it. (Though, not quite in the way the city perceived his guilt.) Philosophy *is* dangerous to the city, and Socrates, who knew what philosophy is, understood that danger as well as and perhaps better than the city did. Furthermore, Socrates obviously did not try for an acquittal. His defense, given the democratic character of the Athenian people, a character Socrates understood, was extremely provocative. Both his provocative defense and his tacit understanding of his guilt pointed to his claim of privilege: the special service that philosophers alone can provide to the polity, the unique blessings conferred by their activity.

Privileges are granted by society on the grounds that in granting these exemptions to the law, society furnishes other benefits, those that are incompatible with the law. Philosophy is at a tension with law because philosophy questions the law. This is very dangerous since a polity is composed of citizens and citizens must be law-abiding. Philosophy can undermine law-abidingness and thus citizenship. On the other hand, philosophy teaches men to pursue excellence, and this can be beneficial, at least to bad or defective polities, for it can improve the characters of the men who make the laws and ultimately the laws themselves. Citizens must be law-abiding, and good laws are the final and irrefutable justification for obedience. In the final analysis, however, the privilege for philosophy rests not on the tolerance of society but on the prudence of the philosopher. He must be cautious, he must be discreet. He must not flagrantly and recklessly attack the laws. Indeed, like Socrates, he must be willing to suffer death at the command of his polity. Socrates went to war at the command of Athens; he died willingly at the command of his city; and this because he was prudent and especially because he was prudent about philosophy. Socrates knew that the highest life, the philosophic life, is possible only within a polity; he knew that philosophy needs the city. The city can exist without philosophy, but philosophy cannot exist without the city.

Law-abidingness is, for ancient thought, prudent and a

nearly perfect duty of all citizens. The exception is an individual privilege that can be claimed by only the rare few.

For the moderns the only exception to the general duty to obey the law is the Lockean right of revolution or, to use more precise Lockean terms, the right to put down a revolt by the government, the right to remedy a usurpation by the government, the right to resist a government that does not protect our natural rights. The true law is the social contract that is made to protect natural rights. The ends or goals of government are permanently foreordained by the social contract. Government itself is merely the agent or means of achieving these predetermined ends. Something or someone must keep the government within these limits, and that task falls upon civil society, which has the right to supervise the fulfillment of the contract and the right to discharge and dismiss the government.

The right of revolution is a collective right not an individual right. It is the right of the society in which the individual participates not his own personal right. The only just revolution is the one supported directly or tacitly by a majority. The individual revolutionary acting as an individual is, in Lockean terms, a mere criminal. His action is not political but anarchical. What this means is that there is no political right of private judgment. No man individually has the right to judge the law and to substitute for it his own opinion, his own belief, his own conscience. To do so is to be a judge in one's own case, but the social contract was formed specifically to preclude this possibility. The social contract was formed to create a common judge. In the state of nature all men possessed the judicial power, and this was a cause of their abject misery. To claim the right of private judgment is to break the social contract; it is to reclaim a right you have alienated and transferred when you made the contract; it is to do what you have already willed and promised not to do. It is a contradiction, an inconsistency and an irrationality. It is irrational in the modern sense of a disservice to one's ultimate personal advantage, for if you can renege, so can everyone else. The contract was made on the grounds that when you alienated your natural right to personal judgment everyone else did the same. To renege is tantamount to willing a return to the state of nature, to the war of the all against the all, to the *summum malum.* Nothing could be more irrational.

Law-abidingness is, for modern contractarian thought, rational and a nearly perfect duty of all citizens. The exception is a collective not an individual right.

The position of the mainstream on the rule of law and the citizen's duty to obey it is that the rule of law is the best way to achieve the ends of government, whether those ends are, as the ancients believed, the goals men ought to pursue, or whether they are, as the moderns believed, the goals men do in fact pursue.

THE PRINCIPLES OF THE MAINSTREAM

The philosophers of the mainstream not only raised the same fundamental questions and examined the same fundamental problems but, despite their profound differences, they agreed on certain fundamental principles. First and foremost, they agreed that there is such a thing as human nature. This is the central concept of the mainstream. Just as the disagreement over whether nature is an end or a beginning, a positive or a negative pole, marks the divergence of ancient and modern thought, so a disagreement over the existence of a human nature, a fixed, definite, fundamental intrinsic character and unchanging core, marks the divergence between the mainstream of Western political thought and its crosscurrent. The crosscurrent, established in the last century, denies the existence of a human nature on the grounds that it is man's "nature" not to have a nature. In its view, human beings are infinitely perfectible, infinitely adaptable, infinitely changeable. Man has no characteristic way that finally prescribes and circumscribes his potentiality. There is no such thing as human nature, according to the philosophers of the crosscurrent. For the philosophers of the mainstream, both ancient and modern, however, there is such a thing as human nature, and this nature is a limitation on being. A limitation on the being called man is diametrically opposed to the principles of the crosscurrent, and so the principle that man has a nature is what distinguishes the more than 2,000-year tradition of the mainstream.

The second major principle of this tradition is that this human nature can be known, that it can be discovered or uncovered by the rational or introspective mind. Thus Socrates, the founder of the Western political tradition, suggested that the proper object of human study is man. Seek to "know thyself" was the advice of Socrates, and this advice was faithfully followed by all the philosophers of the mainstream.

The third major principle of the mainstream is that the nature of man is the standard for measuring all things political. The political community exists for man. The good of individual men is the goal of political life. Man ultimately transcends the political community because he is its rule and measure, he is its goal and purpose. The political community exists for man; it is an instrument of his well-being. Whether it is natural or conventional, whether man is inclined to it or driven toward it, the polity exists to satisfy man's needs, to fulfill his desires, to achieve his purposes, to make possible his happiness.

Fourth, the mainstream agrees that political life is or, more accurately, can be good because when properly constituted it does in fact promote individual human happiness. To live outside the political community is to live improperly and dysfunctionally or briefly and miserably. In a word, it is to live irrationally. Whether reason is calculation of advantage or an understanding of the human good, political life is good and desirable because it is the rational life.

Fifth, the rule of law is a very high thing. Whether law is a substitute for wisdom, the highest and hence the natural title to rule, or whether law is a conventional remedy for a natural defect, for the failure of nature to provide a ruling principle, the rule of law is necessary; it is indispensable to political life.

Sixth, the political man par excellence is the citizen-statesman. The good citizen, the man who plays his political role well, is both law-abiding and a law-giver, hence he is free. He is free because he is a ruler, because he participates in the legislative and judicial functions, because he rules himself, because he is not coerced, because he is not ruled by force, because he obeys laws he has a part in making.

The political philosophers of the mainstream have used the nature of man as a standard to evaluate political things, and they have evaluated political things in order to prescribe remedies for defects, to improve the political life, which they find to be either our to-be-achieved destiny, the terminal excellence predetermined by our nature, or our to-be-secured salvation, the deliverance from the defects of nature. According to the mainstream, Henry Adams was clearly right: "Knowledge of human nature is the *beginning and end* of a political education."

NOTES

CHAPTER 1

1. Plato. *The Republic of Plato.* Trans. Francis MacDonald Cornford, London: Oxford University Press, 1972, pp. 45–53.
2. Ibid., pp. 15–21.
3. Ibid., pp. 42–45.

CHAPTER 2

1. Aristotle. *The Politics of Aristotle.* Trans. Ernest Barker, London: Oxford University Press, 1958, pp. 5–6.
2. Plato. *The Republic of Plato.* Trans. Francis MacDonald Cornford, London: Oxford University Press, 1972, pp. 129–138.
3. Ibid., p. 140.
4. Ibid., pp. 306–317.

CHAPTER 3

1. Aristotle. *The Politics of Aristotle.* Trans. Ernest Barker, London: Oxford University Press, 1958, pp. 5–7.
2. Ibid., p. 1.
3. Ibid.
4. See Aristotle, *The Nicomachean Ethics,* Book X, trans. W. D. Ross, Englewood Cliffs: Prentice-Hall, 1956.
5. Aristotle. *Politics.* pp. 6–7.
6. Ibid., p. 6.
7. Ibid., p. 3.
8. Ibid.
9. Ibid., p. 4.

CHAPTER 4

1. Aristotle. *The Politics of Aristotle.* Trans. Ernest Barker, London: Oxford University Press, 1958, pp. 105–106, 134–136. Plato. *The Republic of Plato.* Trans. Francis MacDonald Cornford, London: Oxford University Press, 1972, pp. 175–179, 217–221.
2. Aristotle. *Politics.* pp. 111, 120, 279–282.
3. Plato. *Republic.* pp. 189–193.
4. Ibid., pp. 195–196.
5. Aristotle. *Politics.* pp. 134–135.
6. Plato. *Apology.* Bound with *Euthyphro* and *Crito,* trans. F. J. Church, Indianapolis: Bobbs-Merrill, 1956, pp. 29–30.
7. Aristotle. *Politics.* pp. 101–106.
8. Ibid., pp. 92–94.
9. Ibid., pp. 101–102.
10. Plato. *Republic.* pp. 102–111; and Aristotle. *Politics.* pp. 11–12, 295–296.
11. Aristotle. *Politics.* pp. 117–120.
12. Aristotle. *Politics.* p. 117.
13. Ibid., p. 118.
14. Ibid., p. 131.
15. Plato. *Republic.* pp. 230–231.
16. Ibid., p. 210.
17. Aristotle. *Politics.* pp. 113–115.
18. Ibid., pp. 115–116.

19. Ibid., pp. 121–123.
20. Ibid., pp. 123–136.
21. Ibid., pp. 123–124.
22. Ibid., pp. 132–136.
23. Ibid., p. 136.
24. Ibid., pp. 140–144.
25. Ibid., pp. 124–127.
26. Ibid., p. 180.
27. Aristotle. *The Nicomachean Ethics,* Book II, trans. W. D. Ross. Englewood Cliffs: Prentice-Hall, 1956.
28. Aristotle. *Politics.* pp. 181–184.
29. Ibid., p. 182.
30. Ibid.
31. Ibid., p. 185.

CHAPTER 5

1. Machiavelli, N. *The Prince.* Bound with *The Discourses,* New York: Modern Library, 1951.
2. Ibid., p. 56.
3. Ibid.
4. Ibid., p. 44.
5. Ibid., pp. 56–57.
6. Ibid., pp. 30, 64.
7. Plato. *The Republic of Plato.* Trans. Francis MacDonald Cornford, London: Oxford University Press, 1972, p. 65.
8. Aristotle. *The Politics of Aristotle.* Trans. Ernest Barker, London: Oxford University Press, 1958, p. 118.
9. Plato. *Apology.* Bound with *Euthyphro* and *Crito,* trans. F. J. Church, Indianapolis: Bobbs-Merrill, 1956, pp. 57–59.
10. Machiavelli, N. *Prince.* pp. 36–37, 70.
11. Ibid., pp. 19–23, 31–32, 57–77.
12. Ibid., pp. 23–24, 91–94.
13. Ibid., pp. 91–94.
14. Ibid., p. 65.
15. Hobbes, T. *Leviathan.* Indianapolis: Bobbs-Merrill, 1958, p. 86.
16. Ibid., pp. 51–53.
17. Ibid., p. 59.
18. Ibid., p. 53.
19. Ibid., p. 61.

CHAPTER 6

1. Hobbes, T. *Leviathan.* Indianapolis: Bobbs-Merrill, 1958, pp. 104–109.
2. Ibid., p. 107. See also p. 86 for Hobbes' rejection of a *summum bonum.*
3. Ibid., p. 106.
4. Ibid., p. 107.
5. Thucydides. *History of the Peloponnesian War.* Trans. Charles Forster Smith, Cambridge: Harvard University Press, 1965, Vol. III, p. 149.
6. Hobbes. *Leviathan.* p. 109.
7. Ibid.
8. Ibid., p. 106.
9. Ibid., p. 105.
10. Ibid., pp. 108, 110.
11. Ibid., pp. 110–111.
12. Ibid.
13. Locke, J. *The Second Treatise of Government.* Indianapolis: Bobbs-Merrill, 1952, p. 4. Emphasis added.
14. Ibid.
15. Ibid., pp. 5–6.
16. Ibid., pp. 6–9.
17. Ibid., p. 6.
18. Ibid., pp. 9, 71.
19. Ibid., pp. 6, 71.
20. Ibid., pp. 9, 71.
21. Ibid., p. 11.
22. Ibid., p. 9.
23. Ibid., p. 12.
24. Ibid., p. 13.
25. Ibid.
26. Ibid., pp. 11–12.
27. Ibid., p. 13.
28. Ibid., p. 17.
29. Ibid.
30. Ibid. pp. 23, 26.
31. Ibid., pp. 24, 27.
32. Ibid., p. 18.
33. Ibid., p. 19.
34. Ibid., pp. 22–28.
35. Ibid., p. 25.
36. Ibid., p. 29.
37. Ibid., p. 25.

38. Rousseau, J.-J. *The First and Second Discourses.* New York: St. Martin's Press, 1964, p. 102.
39. Ibid., pp. 110, 119–121.
40. Ibid., p. 117.
41. Ibid., pp. 116, 117, 119.
42. Ibid., pp. 120–126.
43. Ibid., pp. 115, 127.
44. Ibid., pp. 112, 130–132, 142.
45. Ibid., pp. 113–114.
46. Ibid., pp. 105–107, 115–117, 137.
47. Ibid., pp. 140, 143.
48. Ibid., pp. 143–148.
49. Ibid., p. 149.
50. Ibid., p. 142.
51. Ibid., pp. 154–155.
52. Ibid., p. 141.
53. Ibid.
54. Ibid., pp. 149–156.

Chapter 7

1. Hobbes, T. *Leviathan.* Indianapolis: Bobbs-Merrill, 1958, p. 110.
2. Ibid., p. 112.
3. Ibid., pp. 111–112.
4. Locke, J. *The Second Treatise of Government.* Indianapolis: Bobbs-Merrill, 1952, pp. 54–56, 60; Rousseau, J.-J. *The Social Contract.* Chicago: Henry Regnery, 1954, pp. 8–10.
5. Hobbes. *Leviathan.* pp. 112.
6. Ibid.
7. Ibid., pp. 176–180.
8. Ibid., pp. 143–152.
9. Ibid., pp. 146–147.
10. Locke. *Second Treatise.* pp. 15–17.
11. Ibid., pp. 72–73.
12. Ibid., pp. 60, 73–74.
13. Ibid., pp. 123–125.
14. Ibid., pp. 71–72.
15. Ibid., p. 73.
16. Ibid., pp. 87–88, 126–127.
17. Ibid., p. 129.

18. Hobbes. *Leviathan.* pp. 142–143.
19. Ibid., p. 111.
20. Ibid., pp. 110, 142.
21. Ibid., pp. 115, 120.
22. Ibid., pp. 143–144, 163.
23. Ibid., pp. 150–151.
24. Ibid., p. 169.
25. Ibid., p. 152.
26. Ibid., p. 179.
27. Locke. *Second Treatise.* p. 119.
28. Ibid., pp. 54–55.
29. Ibid., p. 73.
30. Ibid., pp. 76–78.
31. Ibid., pp. 73–74.
32. Ibid., p. 120.
33. Ibid., pp. 84, 123–124.
34. Hobbes. *Leviathan.* pp. 119–120.
35. Rousseau. *Social Contract.* p. 2.
36. Rousseau. *The First and Second Discourses.* New York: St. Martin's Press, 1964, pp. 114–115.
37. Rousseau. *Social Contract.* pp. 10.
38. Rousseau. *Second Discourse.* pp. 154–160.
39. Ibid., p. 162.
40. Ibid., pp. 178–179.
41. Rousseau. *Social Contract.* p. 19.
42. Ibid., pp. 20, 24.
43. Ibid., p. 18.
44. Ibid., p. 24.
45. Ibid., p. 25.
46. Ibid., pp. 26–27.
47. Ibid., pp. 35, 43, 60, 140, 149.
48. Ibid., pp. 66–70, 83.
49. Ibid., p. 149.
50. Rousseau. *Second Discourse.* pp. 89–90.

CHAPTER 8

1. Marx, K. and Engles, F. *Basic Writings on Politics and Philosophy.* Ed. Lewis S. Feuer, New York: Doubleday, 1959, pp. 246–248.
2. Ibid., pp. 247, 262–264.

3. Ibid., pp. 244–245.
4. Ibid., p. 43.
5. Ibid., pp. 249–252.
6. Ibid., pp. 252–254.
7. Marx, K. *Capital.* Trans. Samuel Moore and Edward Aveling, New York: Modern Library, 1906, pp. 708–709.
8. Ibid., pp. 834–837.
9. Marx, K. *Basic Writings.* pp. 255–259.
10. Ibid., p. 247.
11. Ibid., p. 249.
12. Ibid., pp. 17–20.
13. Ibid., pp. 21–29, 256.
14. Nietzsche, F. *The Use and Abuse of History.* Trans. Adrian Collins, Indianapolis: Bobbs-Merrill, 1957, pp. 7–9, 55–56.
15. Ibid., pp. 32, 42, 51–54, 64.
16. Ibid., pp. 61–62.
17. Ibid., p. 21. See also, *Thus Spake Zarathustra* in *The Portable Nietzsche.* Trans. Walter Kaufman, New York: Viking Press, 1968, pp. 126–128.
18. Nietzsche. *Use and Abuse.* pp. 6–7.
19. Ibid., pp. 12–22.
20. Ibid., pp. 8–9.
21. Ibid., pp. 28–30. See also, *Zarathustra,* pp. 129–131.
22. Plato. *The Republic of Plato.* Trans. Francis MacDonald Cornford, London: Oxford University Press, 1972, pp. 227–235.
23. Nietzsche. *Use and Abuse.* p. 70.
24. Ibid., pp. 68–73. See also *Beyond Good and Evil.* Trans. Marianne Cowan, South Bend, Indiana: Gateway, 1955, pp. 42–44, 48–49, 135–137.
25. Nietzsche. *Zarathustra.* pp. 250–253.

SUGGESTED READINGS

CHAPTER 2

1. Aristotle. *Politics.*
2. Plato. *Republic.*

CHAPTER 3

1. Aristotle. *Politics.*
2. Aristotle. *Nicomachean Ethics.*

CHAPTER 4

1. Aristotle. *Politics.*
2. Aristotle. *Nicomachean Ethics.*
3. Plato. *Republic.*

4. Plato. *Laws.*
5. Plato. *Apology* and *Crito.*

CHAPTER 5

1. Machiavelli, Niccolo. *The Prince.*
2. Machiavelli, Niccolo. *The Discourses on the First Ten Books of Titus Livius.*
3. Hobbes, Thomas. *Leviathan.*

CHAPTER 6

1. Hobbes, Thomas. *Leviathan.*
2. Locke, John. *Second Treatise of Government.*
3. Rousseau, Jean-Jacques. *Discourse on the Origin and Foundation of Inequality Among Men.*
4. Rousseau, Jean-Jacques. *Discourse on the Arts and Sciences.*

CHAPTER 7

1. Hobbes, Thomas. *Leviathan.*
2. Locke, John. *Second Treatise of Government.*
3. Rousseau, Jean-Jacques. *Discourse on the Origin and Foundation of Inequality Among Men.*
4. Rousseau, Jean-Jacques. *The Social Contract.*

CHAPTER 8

1. Marx, Karl, and Engles, Friedrich. *The Communist Manifesto.*
2. Marx, Karl and Engles, Friedrich. *The German Ideology.*
3. Marx, Karl. *Capital.*
4. Nietzsche, Friedrich. *The Use and Abuse of History.*
5. Nietzsche, Friedrich. *Beyond Good and Evil.*

INDEX